Great Loss, Greater Love

The Art & Heart of Navigating Grief

By Paula Meyer

Great Loss, Greater Love

The Art and Heart of Navigating Grief

As You Wish Publishing, LLC
Connect@asyouwishpublishing.com

ISBN-13: 978-1-951131-16-6

Library of Congress Control Number: 2021903769

Printed in the United States of America.

Nothing in this book or any affiliations with this book is a substitute for medical or psychological help. If you are needing help please seek it.

Cover graphic by Chris Ayers Creative

Dedicated to my beloved, Gary. The woman I am today is because of your love, trust, and devotion.

Gary Shares: "I am healthy, prosperous, happy, and enjoying our connection to each other and all things."

Acknowledgments

I would like to honor these important people in my life who have stood by me, cheered me on, and loved me greatly: My beautiful mom and traveling partner, Rita; my amazing children Melanie and Trenton; my social media person and biggest cheerleader, Daniela; my editor, Chris; my beloved Dutchies, Richard and Fabienne; my wise mentors, Sunny Dawn Johnston, Susie Carder, and Gina Hatzis; my fabulous Magic Mastery sisters; and my publishers, Kyra and Todd.

Tons of gratitude to those who gifted me places to stay during my travels. Also, my dear friends who have stood by me through thick and thin, you know who you are! And, of course, our beloved animals; Gizmo, Zeus, Xena, Chewie, and Hera. Most importantly, I'm grateful to Spirit for all the gifts.

Table of Contents

Foreword

The book you hold in your hand will rock your world. If you have experienced any kind of loss or hurt, you will be touched. If you've experienced the death of a loved one, a divorce, or a loss of any kind, you will discover your own healing through the journey of my dear friend, Paula.

As I sit here with mascara running down my face, I am blessed to have read and done the work in this book. What started out as a favor to an amazing woman, student, and friend turned into one of the greatest healing processes I could ask for.

I instantly fell in love with Gary, whom I never met. We should all be so lucky to have as great a love as Paula had with Gary, to experience the raw attraction and adoration of two beautiful souls, not perfect but pure. The minute I read the introduction, I started crying. Why am I crying? Why am I feeling this way? Maybe I have some grief to work through? Maybe I have my own loss, my own pain, my own grieving I still needed to do? From the death of my parents to the death and loss of two significant relationships, maybe I have more grief than I even realized.

Each chapter is a symphony of emotions where you see yourself and your own shortcomings. Every page allows you to dig deep into the unknown and what you fear, and how to embrace those fears, your life decisions, and the grace that both Paula and Gary shared for each other and their family.

What a delicious gift to see someone else's struggle, only to reveal your own journey, your own hurts, and your own shortcomings. The beauty in hearing others' stories emerges when you realize you're not alone, that other people have experienced the same hurts and pains you have. To realize that what has been in your way all along has been yourself.

Being able to get the tools of transformation to heal yourself, to seek your answers, is the best gift of all. To peek into someone else's pain only to discover you have your own. This was truly a blessing to my own healing.

We all deserve a journey to heal our hurts, our pains, our successes, and our forever love. Sometimes it takes losing something to appreciate the gift that has been given to us all along. The message I received while being in a friendship with Paula and reading her journey is that gifts are all around you. From the beautiful hummingbird that takes flight, to the bunny that crosses the road. Are you seeing the universal messages that are laid before you, or are you so busy being busy that you miss the gifts that are right in front of you?

I remember when I got married to my children's dad, my grandmother pulled my new husband aside and said, "I don't know why you are marrying her; she doesn't listen."

Where in your life are you not listening or seeing the messages that are all around you? Where are you taking for granted the gifts that are laid at your feet? Mine have been profound. Grandma was right; I am a tough nut! I wait until the freight train has come to run me over to get the lesson! This beautiful story allows you to unwrap the gifts you have been given and appreciate the journey more than the destination!

Oprah was once quoted, "If I had to do it all over again, I would listen to the whisper, not wait until it was a tsunami."

Your story and your experiences are your own, and the gift is the lessons that the world or experience gives us. You can push back, you can deny, or you can embrace the journey and listen to the whispers. For each challenge we encounter, each obstacle we endure, what is the lesson, what is the gift that is wrapped in sandpaper? How can you use these experiences to enrich your life? I have coached thousands of entrepreneurs in living their best, most prosperous life, and one thing I know to be true is that when we can learn from the hardship and the pain, we can live a full and abundant life.

I invite you to live vicariously through Paula and Gary, each on their own miraculous journey of discovery. What you will discover is YOU. What you will discover about yourself is your own suffering and your own breakthroughs. You will discover your own beautiful ending or beginning if you do the work.

I learned that my hardships developed my character, and my pain has given me strength. It didn't consume me; it empowered me. It didn't stop me; it motivated me. It made me a little mad, and when I got mad, I took action. Whatever propels you to decide to heal your past, to heal your hurts, it's worth it!

So read this book as if your life depends on it! Read it and implement the journey. Make it your mission to learn from the lessons the universe is giving you and us. Make your decisions based on your dreams and desires.

So many times, in life, it's too late. We wasted so much time, so much love, so many chances! Listen to Gary speaking the lessons of his own journey to capture the essence of your new beginning. Don't wait until God knocks at your door, and the time to reflect is forced upon you. Decide now to create something unrecognizable and magical for your life, your family's life, or your loved one's life! I want a love that Gary and Paula had, a love of forgiveness and discovery of spirituality that brings my family and my man closer to my pure essence of *love*, forgiveness, and passion.

The journey of what is possible is ready to be explored and created! Dream big, play bold, and create miracles. WE believe in YOU! The journey starts NOW.

Susie Carder

The Profit Coach

Bestselling Author of *Power Your Profits*

Introduction

Gary Shares: "Nothing like dying to make you realize how much you want to live... And how much you cherish life."

Purpose After Loss

How can you move forward with your joy returned after a significant loss?

Finding your purpose after loss is challenging. When you understand there are two types of "busyness" that everyone who has dealt with grief experiences, you can navigate through and beyond your grief more easily.

Two types of busyness happen when you're trying to move forward from a tragic event.

Usually, the first type of busyness is one that just keeps you moving. After my husband Gary died, I noticed that I couldn't sit still. I needed to work and to feel important to someone. Staying busy helped me to feel as though I was accomplishing things.

It's not necessarily productive in the sense of moving forward emotionally or spiritually in your life. However, it can be productive in the sense that you're working at a job earning money or doing things to feel like you're alive. It is also a way to push our feelings down and not deal with them.

If we stay busy enough, we don't have to be continually thinking about our loss.

That kind of busyness is fine in the beginning when you're grieving the loss of people and things that matter. Busyness gives you purpose in that moment of time and allows you to keep moving. It's a good, temporary type of busyness to have. The key word here is *temporary*. At some point, you need to move to a busyness that has purpose, that helps you deal with your emotional crisis, that supports you in creating a meaningful path forward. A purpose that gets you outside of the experience of loss, where your soul can be nurtured, your joy returned, and your life worth living.

The old busyness, in reality, is your old self. It's what you've been taught and conditioned to do. It's an almost unconscious dance of thoughts, behaviors, and actions that we already know how to do. And when a life-changing experience shows up, like a death or a global pandemic, it totally takes over our thinking and our way of life. It's our survival mechanism in action. And when we are thrown into the unknown, we revert to the old busyness that we unconsciously know how to do.

Part of that old busyness might include sharing our story of suffering and pain, repeatedly, to anybody who will listen. And sometimes we share it with people who don't want to hear it, maybe because they've heard it too many times already, or maybe because death is too uncomfortable a topic for them. And either they don't know how to say kindly that they don't want to hear it anymore, or they tell you to get on with it, which can put stress on the relationship, possibly even ending it.

Introduction

My old busyness was to keep my hurt and sadness hidden. That's how I was raised. We didn't talk about emotional things. We were taught to hold our feelings inside and be good and quiet little children, and I carried that into my adult life. So that is the comfortable environment I stayed in after my loss. I hid how I was really feeling and presented the image that my community expected to see. We all have our way of coping, based on how we were brought up. But once we become aware of our default behavior, the door opens to begin moving through it.

Purposeful busyness is the creation of the new you, the creation of your new life, the redefinition of who you want to be, and it's a plan on how to get there. When we finally are ready to move to purposeful busyness as part of our self-re-creation, we must rewrite the story.

The only way we're going to get to that *new self* and that *new life* is with a new story, a new script, a new stage, a new environment, and a new cast of characters who are going to support the new version of ourselves. Now, that's not to say that you must totally change out your tribe or your family, but you do need to surround yourself with people who are willing and able to support the energy and unfoldment of the new version of you.

I'll be sharing stories with you about my year of travel after my husband Gary died from a courageous four-year battle with throat cancer. It's about what I did for myself to move through and move forward in creating my new life. Gary journaled during his illness, and he had always wanted to write a book. And when I began my year of travel, I took along his journal, a beautiful leather-bound journal with a dragonfly on the cover with an old-fashioned lock that I had bought for him when I was strolling through Hyde Park in London. I got myself a beautiful journal with an owl on the cover. The dragonfly was one of Gary's favorite creatures, so I chose that one for him. I also love the symbolism of the dragonfly. It was not only appropriate for Gary's journey, but also for mine once he passed and his journal became my own.

The dragonfly spirit animal symbolizes change and transformation and being open to experience new things. It's usually symbolic of something big unfolding in your personal journey.

The dragonfly also resonates with wisdom and deep thoughts. Dragonflies are not exactly the biggest and strongest creatures in the world, so every flight they take is perilous and unforgettable.

It also symbolizes harmony. When there's strife, work to bring the harmony back. When there's harmony, do your best to keep it with you and share it so that others can benefit from the gifts that harmony brings.

The dragonfly symbolism is an invitation to break away from thoughts and beliefs that are no longer healthy for you. Be open to receive and embrace new ones.

The dragonfly urges you to step out of your comfort zone and embrace your full potential. Break the illusions that prevent you from growing or changing for the better.

Introduction

Some of his last writings are in this journal. He only used the first 32 pages, and I started writing from there. I didn't write every day, just whenever I felt the need. And every so often, I would go back and read what he had written in those 32 pages and marvel at his beautiful handwriting and way of expression. This was my way of keeping his voice alive in my mind and heart. What's so bittersweet about the way that Gary died is that throat cancer is related to the areas of expression in the body, through the throat chakra. Like Gary, many of us are stunted in one way or another throughout our lives, and we can't or won't express ourselves. The reasons are many and varied. For example, we're afraid because growing up, we might have been constantly told to be quiet, we might have been told that what we have to say isn't important, we're embarrassed how our voice sounds, or we're simply afraid to be heard. And sadly, our voice becomes silent.

Expressing himself was one of Gary's biggest challenges during his lifetime. Throat cancer taught him in a very physical way how powerful the mind is and how those thoughts of not having a voice can manifest in the body when we don't temper or redirect them. His illness was so devastating and powerful, and what it did to his ability to speak his truth, his ability to express his emotions, and his capacity to take in nutrition for his body created a deadly experience that ended his life at 62.

It's clear to me now how our spirit and energy can easily wither away while we hide behind silence, with hundreds, if not thousands, of negative thoughts running rampant in our mind. We think if we hide there, no one will see us or hear us, and we don't have to speak up! But what it's really doing is slowly killing us every moment—physically, emotionally, mentally, and spiritually. And weirdly enough, we think that's what we are supposed to do because that's what we've been conditioned to do!

What was so inspiring to me was how he navigated his life after he realized what he had done to his body. He was so aware of how he created his disease and took full responsibility for it, and it was a roadmap for me on how NOT to hold my voice back. How NOT to discount my input. And ultimately about how important it is to express my voice and share my story.

In this book, I'll include portions of Gary's journal ("Gary Shares") for each leg of my year-long journey to all the different places I went to in that year and how I interacted everywhere I went. Partway through the journey, I decided that no matter where I was, I would find these three things each day: Gratitude, Laughter, and the Divine. I called this exercise the "Day Tripper Challenge." I journaled about them and shared them with my Facebook tribe. In doing this, I was expressing in two ways: firstly, through the written word, which allows the negative energy to be released from my physical body and then be replaced with life-affirming energy; and secondly, through my tribe, by being a witness to the beautiful things in life. This ultimately helped me to map the process in my mind, that every day, there is *always* something to be grateful for, *always* something to have a good belly laugh about, and *always* something truly divine if we open our hearts and see. It's so easy, right? Simplicity is the key! Then, I'll finish each chapter with a flashback from my life with Gary, the gifts I've received, and finally, an insightful activity for you to do to help you map the process in your brain!

Now that is *purposeful busyness*! This easy process supported my journey through grief into happiness and joy. It can work for any form of grief, not just the death of a loved one. It can help you too! And you don't have to travel the world to put this into action. You can look for these three things every day, no matter where you are. Get yourself a journal and use it for all the activities in this book. Journaling is an amazing tool to help you get your feelings out, release negative emotional energy, develop your intuition, and provide a way for creative insights and ideas to come forth.

There's one more thing that's especially important to remember about grief: it doesn't ever completely go away. It will show up at certain times depending on what's going on in your life. Your job is to take those tools that you've learned and used at the beginning of your grief journey and continue to use them to keep moving through and forward. Eventually, if you keep up the work, you'll find that the grief isn't as painful as it used to be. That it doesn't always make you cry. And sometimes it will make you laugh and remember all the amazing and fun things about the person who died. Or the marriage that ended. Or the job you left. Or the people who fell away. Or the global pandemic that rocked our world in 2020.

And isn't life all about evolution? Join me, and let's have fun discovering who we truly are and how beautiful and amazing life is. Life is for everyone, NO EXCEPTIONS!

Come on, let's hit the road!

Chapter 1
Who Am I Now?

Gary Shares: "I am a powerhouse of potentials waiting to be expressed."

For me, my new version when Gary died was *Paula without Gary*. The big question was, how do I create that life and still be happy and fulfilled?

Unpacking the Old

Four months after Gary passed, a friend suggested that I consider grief counseling. I've never been a fan of talk therapy, given my fear of expression, but I knew that I needed some help. Grief is a very heavy emotion and can easily create havoc in mind and body if not addressed. The only thing I was sure of was that I wanted a grief coach who was also a widow. I just felt that I needed someone with the same experience coaching me. Once I set that intention, the Universe sent a coach very quickly, and I began an online grief program. It was supposed to take eight weeks, but due to my heavy travel schedule, it ended up taking me four months! In hindsight, I believe that I sabotaged myself by using the excuse that I was too busy. However, I celebrated myself for finally completing it in February 2019, and I continued to work with my grief coach through April of 2020.

My self-development training over the years gave me a solid foundation to start with, but the grief coaching was the tool helping me move through and forward. We cannot do this on our own. We need a tribe supporting us. I think back to our ancestors, who were so much more comfortable with death and dying. They celebrated the elderly and ill, compassionately caring for them through illness and death. They then loved and honored the family left behind so that, in essence, no one was ever left behind.

Working with my grief coach helped me to begin healing myself from within. She shined a light for me that illuminated possibilities for a fulfilled and purposeful life without Gary. I found that joy and happiness were still available to me. That I needed to put myself first and take responsibility for creating my new life. Being a young widow at 54, I knew that I potentially had a good 25-30 years of life left to live. That was more time than I had with Gary! I certainly didn't want to live the rest of my life in pain and sorrow. I gained the courage to step into that new future, to surrender to the Divine, and to have faith that the Universe is always on my side, always supporting me, and never letting me fall without catching me.

At the end of 2018, I was a mess. My health had deteriorated, and I had an emergency appendectomy. I had lost 30 pounds by the time the year ended. I was exhausted and drained yet continued to work obsessively to avoid dealing with my grief. **(Old Busyness)**

I believe that the grueling physical and mental challenges of my job, compounded by grief, caused my appendicitis.

Chapter 1 | Who Am I Now?

As 2019 rolled in, I made the choice to leave the job I loved, working with people I adored, supporting people in their spiritual growth, with wonderful and amazing travel experiences around the globe. You might wonder, why would anyone in their right mind want to leave that? What I found for me was that this job was the old type of busyness that we discussed earlier. It was the type of busyness that, while it was supporting and celebrating other people in their spiritual growth, there was no time for re-creating the new me after Gary died. To have that time for myself, I had to choose myself. And believe me, choosing me was extremely hard.

As women, we're brought up to believe that everybody else comes before us. As a wife, a mother, a daughter, we take that act of selflessness within our families and extend it out into our world, into our work life, and into our community life. We very rarely bring that inward to support ourselves. It becomes glaringly evident in the face of trauma because we then find that we don't have the foundation inside us to **get through and create something new**. We are just told to do the best we can with what we have, be grateful for what we got, suck it up and figure it out. And that's damn hard when you're going through the aftermath of a tragedy, regardless of its magnitude.

And even worse, I was creating disease and disorder in my body.

Being a caregiver is hard. Being a caregiver for someone you love is extremely hard. Being a caregiver for someone you love and working a full-time job is brutal on your body and mind. I wish I had realized the toll this would take on me. You would think that after being on the self-development train since 1997, I would have been prepared for this. I know what unchecked thoughts can do to the body—that's how disease is created. Gary and I learned this together during his illness, and up until the end of his life, he was addressing the underlying issues that caused his throat cancer, which were about expression and self-worth. Even though he died, his efforts did have an effect. His energy is still very much present and supporting our family and me in expressing our voices by sharing our wisdom and experience for the highest good.

What I was missing during Gary's illness was the importance of love and compassion for myself. I was so caught up in using every waking moment to care for him or tend to my work that I never made time for myself. I believed that in being selfless in this way, I would be fine. That all the good I was doing for others would carry over into my health and wellness by osmosis. The truth is that I was in severe denial. I kept my mind crazy busy, so I didn't have to think about his approaching death. I dismissed my intuition and the signals from my body. I had several tests done that indicated two areas for concern that I ignored. I could not see that I was worn out, physically, mentally, and emotionally. When those in my inner circle asked, I always assured them that I was fine.

After Gary died on a Friday, my boss asked me on Saturday if I needed to take some time off. My answer: *"Absolutely NOT! I need to keep moving forward. I will be back to the office on Monday."* The Sunday after Gary died, we got the devastating news that my ex-husband, Brad, the father of my two children, had died unexpectedly at 58. I got angry at my ex-husband, asking him how he could die now, so soon after Gary? As if he was stealing Gary's thunder! I quickly apologized to him and asked Gary to check on him and see that he arrived okay! Maybe Gary could take him golfing in heaven, as they were both ardent golfers.

And then, true to my word, I was back to work on Monday. When I wasn't eating or sleeping, which wasn't much, I was working obsessively to keep my mind occupied. Colleagues around the world would marvel that I was answering and sending emails at all hours of the day and night.

What I have since learned is that the survival centers in the physical body (the first three chakras or energy centers) are where our intuition or "gut feelings" first present themselves. When we continue to ignore them, they manifest as pain in the body. I knew this from all my years of study, but I didn't really "know" it. I wasn't eating or sleeping well, and I was having digestive issues, painful side aches, and lower back pain. I thought I was moving forward, but instead was very rapidly moving backward. Five months later, on my 55th birthday, I was in the ER having an emergency appendectomy. Still, I didn't stop. I sent my son to the office to pick up my laptop so I could keep working in the hospital. I insisted to my boss that I would be able to travel in two days to the UK!

When I finally realized that my body was not well enough to go, I set my focus on the next trip to Mexico a few weeks later. Not even an emergency appendectomy was slowing me down in dealing with my loss or my health. In retrospect, I'm thankful that this did not happen in a foreign country or on an airplane. I had just returned several days earlier from a business trip to Australia. Somebody was looking out for me and made sure I was home when the emergency happened!

A month later, the Mexico event went very well, however, not without some additional physical challenges for me, including a fall onto my hip that left a softball-size bruise and increased back and neck pain. I lost another twenty pounds by Christmas. More clues from the universe to slow down! Finally, when I was on vacation in Denver during the holidays, I realized that I couldn't keep going. I had a long conversation with my mom. We made a pact. If I retired early from my job, she would retire from hers, and we would begin a year of travel!

I wasn't 100% sure about this travel plan. However, after a particularly stressful day at work, I called my boss and had a meltdown. I'm sure I probably frightened him a bit, considering my usual calm and cool persona. He was gracious and understanding, and he worked with me to wind things down so I could finally put myself first and begin my healing journey. I'm forever grateful for his support, as it was not an easy feat to transition everything, especially with a busy new year starting.

I discovered that the only way that I was going to move forward into a happy, joyful life without Gary was to set everything else aside and give my full attention to ME. That was the only way I was going to survive. I did not want to go on living hiding behind a mask, as a smaller and smaller version of myself. And I didn't want to be labeled as a sad, lonely widow. Or for people to feel sorry for me and think my life had less meaning because there was one less person in it.

An unfortunate thing about death for those left behind is they not only lose the person they love, but many also lose people around them who don't know how to stay connected without the person who died. So rather than going through the uncomfortableness of creating a different relationship because of the fear of causing more sadness and the fear of coming face-to-face with our own mortality, it's easier to just fade away. Sadly, many family and friends slowly dissolve into the background, and some eventually disappear altogether.

This throws another wrinkle into the equation. Not only have you lost your loved one and the way of life they represented for you, but you've also lost other important people around you because of the fear of death. Now you're also grieving the loss of small or large parts of your community and trying to figure out a way to survive that as well. You already feel less than whole with the original loss, and then the subsequent fading away of others only increases the feeling of being lesser.

The very same thing can happen with divorce, leaving your job, a global pandemic, moving away from your community, or being physically or verbally abused. It can be any event, big or small, that separates us from our known and comfortable environment and causes us to grieve deeply.

Activity: Who Am I Now?

- What story are you telling now? Are you the victim or the victor?
- What three thoughts constantly run through your mind?
- How do these thoughts make you feel?
- Do you believe these thoughts?
- Journal about it for 15 minutes.

Gratitude, Laughter, Divine

Think about today, and answer these questions in your journal:

- What are you grateful for today?
- What made you laugh today?
- Did you feel the Divine today?

Chapter 2
Packing the New

Gary Shares: "I am open minded and moving more and more to a heart-centered joyful being."

It becomes so important that you dig deep within, love yourself, and realize the truth of who you are. We are all children of God, we all have value, we all have a voice that matters and deserves to be heard. We've got to find our own internal resources, ask for help, and figure out how to emerge into this new person who's waiting to be birthed. When you have the courage to do that, to change your circumstances, to change your environment, to accept that we are solely responsible for our happiness, the universe sees your effort and rewards you with a whole new tribe of people who are more than willing to support, encourage, and love the new person who is emerging.

And so began my year of travel! Traveling was a balm for my wounded soul. It allowed me to see myself in different environments, around different people, and immersed in many kinds of amazing energy. I was able to begin creating a new life that was still fun and joyful without Gary. And as moments of sadness and grief arose, I found ways to accept it, love into it, find the gifts within it, and move forward.

On my journey, I have met many amazing people whom I would never have met in my life with Gary. I'm grateful for the things that have come out of his death. For the people who have shown up. The experiences that have developed. The opportunities that have presented themselves. None of these, *let me repeat that: none of these* could have happened in my life WITH Gary. I know that's a scary thought, and it can feel a bit like dishonoring the person who's gone. But I believe that we come together in this life with the people who are in it to learn new things and have new experiences to further the development of our soul. I believe Gary was here to help me on my spiritual journey. I was not on any kind of spiritual path when I met him, and what drew me to him was his spirituality.

To be honest, I fell into learning about his spirituality because he was so damn handsome! I was willing to learn about it to be his girl! Apparently, he had to come into this life as super handsome, so I would be willing to listen and learn about spirituality! Part of his work, then, was to support me on my spiritual path as a mentor, a teacher, a friend, and a lover, to show me the magnificence of who I am AND the power of who I am. He accomplished what he was supposed to as far as our interactions in this life. More importantly, he accomplished what he needed for his own evolvement. Now he's on to bigger and better things to further his soul development.

My job now is to further my own soul development, on my own and in full knowledge of my own power. I can say this now but surely couldn't have said it two years ago: I am profoundly grateful for the gift of Gary's death. The Paula I am now was simply not possible before. My life with Gary was to prepare me to become the Paula I am now, and my job is to honor what he was here to teach me, and to take that information, that learning, and that energy and love, and propel myself forward into my new life. I spent the last several months of Gary's life being his caregiver. I needed to learn about intense caregiving and how to just give love and care while watching him slowly diminish in front of my eyes. To see his body disintegrate while all of his vitality and zest for life was gradually leaving. There was truly a gift in witnessing that, to really appreciate my health, my life, my family and friends, and my freedom to live this new life in a way that supports my greatest good.

When I left my job in February 2019, I promised myself I would focus on myself. I would travel the world and really enjoy and be present in all the places that I visited. I would travel with family and friends and really enjoy them and be present with them. And I would travel with myself and be completely transparent, present, and loving to the most important person in my life, ME!

Flashback: In the Beginning

I met Gary at the hotel where he worked, the Doubletree Hotel in Tukwila, Washington, when my employer held an event there. When the event was over, we had a celebration cocktail party, and Gary was the bartender. He was so handsome, just my type, tall, with blonde hair and blue eyes. My friends dared me to go up and talk to him. Though I was a very shy person when it came to men, I'd had a bit to drink, and my confidence was high. I went to the bar and confidently ordered a margarita. He made the drink, and I was too nervous to really say anything. I took the drink and went back to my friends. I was about halfway through the drink when a few minutes later, he appeared with another drink. He said that he had made the wrong drink! I hadn't even noticed! I was so excited just to have connected with him, I didn't even realize that the drink was wrong! I didn't talk to him the rest of the evening, and at the end of the party, I walked out to the lobby and there he was! I was so surprised to see him. He told me that he left when his shift was over and then decided to come back to see if he could find me. We decided to go to another bar and have a few more drinks. And the rest is history!

As I got to know him over the next few months, aside from his striking good looks, what was even more intriguing was his spirituality and his story of healing his back from a devastating fall that should have left him paralyzed. As the story goes, back in the late 80s, he and his friend were out partying, and they came back to his apartment in the wee hours of the morning with no keys. Even though he was afraid of heights, in his alcohol-induced bravado, he decided to climb up to the balcony on the second floor. As he was getting ready to swing his leg over the railing, it broke. He fell to the ground and landed on his back. He was fully conscious the whole time, and when he hit the ground, he knew that his back was broken. He did not immediately go to the hospital as he didn't have faith in mainstream medicine. I don't recall exactly how much time elapsed before he knew he needed medical attention, and he ended up at the ER. He had Harrington Rods put into his back to stabilize his spine.

He had always wanted to write a book about the experience of his injury and his miraculous healing. He had always doubted himself and lacked confidence in his voice and telling his story. Even as miraculous as the story was, he couldn't get past the emotional strangulation of his voice during his childhood. Gary was born in Minnesota in 1955 to an unwed mother. As was common during that era, her family quietly sent her away to the city to have the baby. Not long after that, he and his mom were on a train to Seattle. After arriving, she met a man that she would marry and have three more children with. Gary didn't know that this man wasn't his real father until one fateful day as a teenager, he found documentation revealing that the man he had grown up with was not his biological father. It was a shocking revelation and one that was never resolved in his lifetime. He never learned who his real father was, as his mother refused to divulge the truth about his parentage. This refusal was disconcerting in many ways, creating many crazy ideas in his head about why it was such a secret. What could be so bad that his mother could not share it with him? Years later, he told me that growing up, he always felt that something was not quite right, as his stepfather distanced himself from Gary, which he did not do with his other siblings. Not knowing the truth and based on how he was brought up, he turned it inward on himself and created the story that he didn't have anything worthy to say or share with anyone, and slowly faded away into silence, sadness, and anger.

In this book, I plan to share his story because I think there's a great story there. I want to write the story for him, the story that he was never able to write for himself. Prior to his accident, he was beginning to delve into metaphysical studies, meditation, and healing practices. He believed he could heal himself, so he got pictures of a healthy spine and put them on his wall where he could see them every day. He envisioned in his mind his perfect spine. He would close his eyes and picture himself running through the forest. He would feel the breeze blowing through his hair as he ran at full speed. He could smell the strong, sweet smell of the forest. Every time he did this, he imagined and experienced everything in such exacting detail that all his senses were heightened and alive, just as if he were physically having the experience. This way of healing and creating came to him through his meditation practice. Someone or something from beyond was instructing him on exactly what he needed to do. Every day, he spent time visualizing his spine perfectly healed as he ran through the forest.

After the surgery, he was put in a body cast, which he wore to stabilize his spine and help in the healing process. He checked himself out of the hospital early, against his doctor's wishes, and embarked on a road trip in his Volkswagen bus. He started his journey in San Diego, where he lived at the time, and went to New Mexico, Arizona, and Colorado in search of healers.

He met up with many amazing healers, and one of the more notable ones was in a place called Ojo Caliente in New Mexico. This man is now a well-known speaker and teacher with nearly 30 books in his long career, but this was back in the day when he was first starting out. When Gary met with him, the healer asked about his old Indian friend. Gary didn't understand what he was talking about, and the healer told him that he had an old Indian spirit that was with him all the time. This spirit told the healer to tell Gary about push-starting his VW bus. Gary was so surprised because there was no way he could have known that's how he started his VW bus! He was always parking it on a hill to push start it

14

easily! So, Gary learned he had help from the Spirit realm in his healing process!

Gary's ultimate goal was to heal his back completely and have the Harrington Rods removed, which is not something that typically happens with this type of surgery. But he was adamant that this was going to happen. Over time, a miraculous thing occurred. He said he just knew everything was healed, and he set out to find a surgeon who would remove the rods. Of course, it was tough to find a surgeon willing to remove them because usually, Harrington Rods are a permanent thing. He drew to him a young orthopedic surgeon at Swedish Hospital in Seattle who was willing to do it. When the surgery was done on March 7, 1989, the surgeon told Gary that he was shocked to see how everything looked around the site of the initial injury and surgery. Where the first surgeon said it looked like a mess of spaghetti, everything was now perfectly healed, as it should be in a healthy body!

I was intrigued by the story of his healing. I had never heard anything like this. I was not on any kind of spiritual journey, and it was so new to me that something like this could be done. The long scar down the back of his spine was proof of the miracle and the fact that once the rods were removed, he could do anything that a normal healthy back would allow a person to do. He had many physically intensive jobs over the years following the removal of the rods. He loved landscaping and created beautiful stone walls and garden beds at our home. You would never know that he had a serious back injury. Our yard was a testament to his talent to create beautiful grounds and amazing rockeries. I used to tease him that he was a builder of the pyramids in a past life, as he was so adept at working with stones.

In our 20+ years together, we continued our spiritual path. I had two young children from my first marriage, and the aftermath of the divorce, child custody issues, and step-parenting was a huge mountain to climb. Most times, it didn't feel like we ever got past the foothills! The greatest challenge for both of us was using our voices. We were so similar in that way that many times it was a struggle to communicate, not only with each other but also with our children and my ex-husband. We nearly broke up three times in those first ten years. I honestly don't know how we managed to stay together. I guess Spirit had other plans for us!

Over the years, Gary developed a great relationship with my son. Gary stepped up when my son's father stepped out of his life for a few years. One of Gary's fondest moments was when our son told him that he considered him his real dad. And when his father came back into his life, Gary encouraged him to develop a new connection. I'm grateful that our son got the opportunity to mend fences and have a meaningful relationship with his father before he died.

My daughter and Gary had a difficult relationship. She remembered her father and me together, where my son didn't, so it was harder for her to connect with Gary. It didn't help that I made it difficult by not allowing Gary to be more of a parent with her. I was trying to protect her from more pain by giving her more time and attention than I gave anyone else. After she had grown up and moved to Tucson and then Jacksonville, their relationship improved and toward the end of his life, they had become closer. My daughter shared with me recently that Gary had apologized to her for their tough times when she was home. She was so grateful for that!

When our son left for college in 2012, we both worried about how we would do on our own. We had never been together without the kids. We didn't know each other without the kids. What happened was a game-changer. We got to really know each other and decided that we still genuinely loved each other! Around this time, I had started to travel more for work, and Gary began coming with me on many of my trips around the world. Exploring new lands, new cultures, and meeting new people together was a great way to learn about each other and to appreciate the blessings of each other individually and as a couple.

We had two amazing years. Then the walls came tumbling down when cancer invaded our tranquil world.

Activity: Journaling Awareness

Think about how Gary healed himself from his back injury.

- Do you believe your thoughts or beliefs can create illness in the body?
- Do you believe you have the power to create optimum health?
- Think about a past health challenge you had.
- What was happening in your life at the time it happened?
- What thoughts were you thinking?

- If it's no longer an issue, how did it change? What did you do?
- If it's still an issue, are you still thinking the same thoughts? Are you in the same environment?

Gratitude, Laughter, Divine

Think about today, and answer these questions in your journal:

- What are you grateful for today?
- What made you laugh today?
- Did you feel the Divine today?

Chapter 3
Leg 1: Early March 2019

Gary Shares: "I can change my circumstances and co-create a new amazing reality."

Finally, all the planning and creating for my year of travel was about to begin! All the days, weeks, and months of stressing about it were finally over. The excitement and energy were palpable. I had not been this excited about anything for a long time. I would begin my year of travel on a solo trip to Arizona to visit some beloved friends in Phoenix and Sedona and to attend the Celebrate Your Life International Women's Summit.

On March 3rd, the day before setting off on my journey, I enjoyed a visit from a hummingbird in the early afternoon. I gratefully watched it land on the feeder and drink as the sun shone through the blue-colored glass and glinted off the metal base of red flowers. Most of the time, hummingbirds flutter their wings as they drink from the feeder, but this one rested its wings while it drank. It occasionally stopped to look up and survey the landscape, a backdrop with so many shades of green: evergreen trees, maple trees, and grass. It was the perfect way to be sent off, as if Gary were there to do the bon voyage honors in the form of this beautiful creature. I ended the evening relaxing with my son by a roaring fire in the fire pit just below the front yard. This was a treasured family custom that Gary and I had carried on through the years: watching my son start the fire, just as Gary had done so many times before, with the propane torch emitting its jet engine sound and bright blue flame. Watching the brilliant gold and orange flames engulfing and dancing amidst the wood and branches as they crackled and shot sparks upwards. Contemplating as the white and gray smoke was billowing toward the night sky was another bittersweet yet wonderful way to begin this new chapter.

I landed in Phoenix to beautiful weather and picked up my rental car, a white Ford Fiesta with Nevada license plates. I found it interesting that the license plate number, 362-G31, consisted of all numbers and just one letter, a G! And Gary's age at the time of his death was there also, 62! This Nevada-registered rental car in Arizona, with the synchronistic plate number, was the perfect car for the first leg of my trip!

I drove to my new digs for the next week to be with my wonderful hosts, who had graciously invited me to stay with them in their beautiful home. Their plan was for me to be pampered and loved! It was perfect that I was able to time it with the International Women's Summit the following weekend. There were many fun times, and my friends truly provided wonderful R&R for this sad and wounded soul. I ended the day in a gorgeous guest room with amazing artwork on all the walls, a comfy bed, a sitting area, and my own bathroom. The best part, though, was the painting on the wall outside the bedroom: Wonder Woman. I had been nicknamed Wonder Woman by former colleagues, one of whom had created an image of my face superimposed on Linda Carter's Wonder Woman, which I treasure to this day! The painting was quite a warm welcome and a reminder of how powerful I was being by taking this step into my brave new world.

The next afternoon, my friends invited me to join them for the Choco Challenge by Fuego Box, which they were videotaping to send in to support the fight against prostate cancer. They had witnessed Kristen Bell and Dax Shepard take the challenge on the Ellen Show, where they had been in the audience. They doubted that the spicy chocolate was as bad as Kristen and Dax made it out to be. We had remedies ready to combat the potential consequences of the spicy chocolate: tequila, yogurt, milk, water, and lots of Kleenex. My friend in charge of this experience, our esteemed emcee, ate the entire piece in one bite, while the rest of us ate tiny bites and didn't finish. Let me just say that it was extremely hot and spicy chocolate. The sixteen-minute video that was submitted was totally hilarious. To watch my friend who ate the whole piece, even now, makes me laugh out loud! Such a fond memory of good and spicy times with great and spicy friends. Enjoy the video here: https://vimeo.com/321587613. I recently got a video from them reminiscing and laughing about it, and my friend said it took him days to begin to feel better. I'm surprised he was able to do all the things we did in the days that followed the infamous Choco Challenge.

Later, we went to Taliesin West, Frank Lloyd Wright's desert laboratory and school of architecture. As we toured this amazing creation in the desert foothills of the McDowell Mountains in Scottsdale, I was inspired not just by its simplicity but also the majestic quality of the buildings and how they blended in so beautifully with the desert landscape. Asian artwork, metal sculptures, and statues were placed throughout the grounds. There was an intriguing circular doorway built into the rock garden wall that was an entryway into another part of the garden. With stone pavers leading up to it and graced by a beautiful red wooden circular door, it felt like you could enter through that portal into a magical realm beyond. It was so simple and yet so powerful, almost as if Wright wanted you to feel what it feels like to mystically walk through walls. I felt as if this was an invitation from the Divine, leading me into my new life.

As I did further research into Wright, considered the greatest American architect of all time, I found this intriguing quote by him in 1957: *"The mission of an architect is to help people understand how to make life more beautiful, the world a better one for living in, and to give reason, rhyme, and meaning to life."*

I had heard of him years before but didn't really know much about him other than that he was a celebrated architect of modern style buildings. Honestly, I didn't really get his vision or style. I loved these pearls from his website that, along with visiting Taliesin, brought him to life for me, gave me a much greater appreciation for his genius, and allowed me to see in a deeper way the connection of people, nature, and buildings:

"Above all integrity," he would say: "buildings like people must first be sincere, must be true."

"In organic architecture then, it is quite impossible to consider the building as one thing, its furnishings another and its setting and environment still another," he concluded. "The spirit in which these buildings are conceived sees all these together at work as one thing."

I believe this put me in a better state of mind for my year of travel, as it gave me a big picture perspective of learning about and truly experiencing all the places that were on my itinerary for the coming year.

Reflecting back to the Wonder Woman painting, this was a precursor to all the amazing women I would see at the upcoming International Women's Summit. I had the pleasure of seeing these ladies speak, and most for the first time: Liz Gilbert, Lisa Nichols, Sunny Dawn Johnston, Denise Linn, Laverne Cox, Gina Hatzis, and many others.

I was blown away by all the powerful women speakers! I had never been in a room with so many amazing women, listening to so many powerful feminine voices! I spent 35 years of my career working for and in the shadow of men, and I had forgotten how powerful women can be. I came out of this event with huge enthusiasm for women's empowerment. It accelerated my healing by reminding me how powerful I am, that my life is my responsibility, and it is completely up to me how I create it from this point forward.

My soul was ignited, and something in me said that I was on the right track. All of us in attendance were nourished, loved, celebrated, and honored throughout the weekend. We experienced great lectures, workshops, Q&A sessions, wonderful meals, daily dancing, a high-energy party, a wonderful array of vendors, and even a toe-reading! Sometime before this event, I decided to participate in a collaborative book with As You Wish Publishing, who was also at this event, and I got to witness my future publisher in action! I just knew that this was my tribe, and I committed and submitted my application on March 14 to write a chapter in *Inspirations: 101 Uplifting Stories for Daily Happiness.*

The day the summit ended, my hosts took me to Cosanti Gallery in Paradise Valley, the gallery and studio of Italian American architect Paolo Soleri. Here they make handcrafted, one-of-a-kind bronze wind bells, each with a unique color pattern, hand-carved motif, luminosity, and sound. As we walked through the manufacturing section, it felt like we were on another planet, so unique were the buildings and surroundings. And when you walked into the section where all the bells were displayed, it was almost overwhelming to see all the different styles and sizes. I selected two bells. It was difficult to choose, yet these two bells are unique reminders of wonderful, unique, and generous friends.

On the afternoon of March 11th, I packed my bags, loaded up the car, and bade a fond farewell to my wonderful friends. I drove up I-79 and the Red Rock Scenic Byway to Sedona. It was a cloudy and cold day, yet the majestic landscape of the red rock formations of Sedona made the clouds and cold irrelevant. Another beloved friend had booked me a room at the beautiful Hilton at Bell Rock on the top floor with a beautiful view. I was in for another treat!

The next day we took a day trip to Jerome, a small historic copper-mining town near Sedona, named the *Wickedest Town in the West.* In its heyday in the 1920s, its population peaked at nearly 15,000. Today, it's a small historic boutique town with around 50-100 residents. One of the highlights was a museum that had a section for the history of prostitution in the town. Here are some excerpts from *The Hierarchy of Prostitution* display that I found educational, intriguing, and quite humorous, and typed exactly as written.

Brothels: Were for the working men. They could be located in a saloon or an apartment building. The atmosphere of each establishment varied. Sometimes a man called the "professor" would play the piano and serve as a bouncer. Meals could be provided, along with the other "comforts of home."

Parlor Houses: Were high-end establishments. The women were experienced, had luxurious living conditions, and made easy money. For men, it was like visiting gentility. There would be fine music, decorations, food, and drink. Personal entertainment would be handled in a most discreet manner; it was more like a social call. The girls would be pretty and intent on the quality of encounters, not the quantity.

Independent Contractor: A prostitute could work alone in a house, shack, or cottage. She had the freedom to pick her own clients. But the particular danger of the situation was that she had no one to protect her, and there was always a threat of uninterrupted violence.

Red Light District: This term originated when the men who worked for the railroads left their red lanterns in front of places of prostitution so that they could be found in case of an emergency. Displaying a red light, curtains, or a shade in front of establishments later became law in many cities.

This is quite an interesting example of the power levels of women in the business of prostitution. It's not so different from the hierarchies in our current business world with which women still deal today.

The following day, I was taken to meet up with a shaman for a two-hour Vortex Spiritual Land Tour. We left in his car, and as we were leaving, we saw a rabbit under a nearby car on the driver's side. He shared that all animals that cross our paths are sent to us for a reason, and this rabbit indicated new beginnings for me. The fact that it was sitting under the car on the driver's side indicated that I was in control of my new future. As we drove on, he asked me what my two favorite animals were. I said an eagle and an owl. He told me that eagles signify the ability to see everything from a higher view, to see the bigger picture. He continued that owls have the added ability to see a full 360 degrees without altering the direction of their bodies, which signifies the ability to see things from any perspective. He reminded me to always watch and listen for ways that nature presents itself, especially with wild animals, as we can learn a lot from them based on their spiritual significance.

We reached our first destination, Rachel's Knoll, an incredible spot high up in the hills, to view the magnificent beauty and awe-inspiring landscape of West Sedona. As the shaman walked me around this beautiful area, he led me through various exercises to honor my late husband and to soothe my grief at his loss. He presented me with an arrowhead and asked me to hold it in my hand. I was encouraged to share about Gary and what I appreciated most about him. In sharing, the tears welled up, and he offered me a Kleenex to wipe the tears. Then we buried those tears in the sacred ground, giving them back to the earth.

We walked a little further and stopped to see various juniper trees whose trunks had been contorted by the vortex of energies in the area. He said this was nature's example of how our bodies do the same things with the energies that we surround ourselves with in our lives. Our bodies are meant to sway and be flexible through the vortices of life. When we resist, that is what causes pain and disease. The trick, he said, was to be conscious and aware through this flexibility and be an active participant in melding our mind and bodies, rather than being molded unconsciously.

We came to an incredibly twisted tree on the edge of the cliff. He instructed me to place the arrowhead that I held in my hands as I shared about Gary into a crevice in the tree. We had a moment of silence as we honored Gary's life. He gave me another arrowhead to take home as a remembrance of the day. He gave Gary an honorary Native American name, Gary White Cloud. He took my phone and walked over to the next cliff and took several pictures of me, silhouetted against the rocks and the puffy-clouded blue sky, as I raised my arms up in celebration and joy.

Our next stop was the Amitabha Stupa & Peace Park. Here I got to see a Buddhist Stupa and prayer wheels for the first time. There was a beautiful wooden Buddha that sat just beyond the stupa. We walked to a creek further up the path where we passed a cactus that was shaped like a heart. He allowed me to pick a feather from his collection. I chose a gray feather with blue twine wrapped around the base. He told me a gray feather signified communication, and the blue signified being "true blue." We burned the feather as an offering to Spirit. There was a small part left that he instructed me to take home and burn when it felt right.

As we made our way back, I asked if it was okay to put some of Gary's ashes into the creek. We stopped, and I spread a small amount in the crystal-clear water that was streaming over the beautiful red rocks. We then came upon a medicine wheel, and as I stood in the center, he walked around the perimeter with his sacred drum. He drummed a steady beat as I turned to face him at each compass point as he walked around the wheel. We finished this ceremony, me in the center with the drum, to do my own drumming. We headed back past the Buddha and the stupa to the prayer wheels, where we spun the wheels and completed our sacred tour.

My visit with the shaman was such a wonderful way to end my Arizona trip. As a final celebration, we had hors d'oeuvres and wine at Mariposa with many more friends. The next day, I had one last lunch with my dear friend at the Sedona Golf Resort, with a spectacular view of the red rocks of Sedona. Then I was on my way back to Phoenix to catch my flight back home.

Momma arrived on March 16th in preparation for our Alaska trip for a dog-sledding tour and then our road trip across the country. My son had planned to move home in July 2018 from Tucson to help take care of Gary and was sadly not able to make that happen before he passed. He had two big huskies, Zeus & Xena, who moved home with him a month after Gary died. Because of his love for his huskies, I gave him the dog-sledding tour as a Christmas gift.

On March 20th, we boarded our flight at SeaTac airport to Anchorage, Alaska. As I was playing my favorite airplane game, Monkey Wrench, one of the answers was the song *North to Alaska*! A good sign! Anchorage was overcast and cold when we arrived, yet serene and peaceful. We had planned to do an Aurora Borealis tour the next day, but the weather was not cooperating, so we opted to visit an animal sanctuary instead. We saw moose, buffalo, bears, elk, wolves, eagles, owls, and the cutest porcupine who climbed up the sides of his cage, so intent on connecting with his visitors.

The next morning, we got up early for the big day! We stopped at a restaurant in Talkeetna and found this Mark Twain quote on our table: *"Travel is fatal to prejudice, bigotry, and narrow-mindedness, and many of our people need it sorely on these accounts. Broad, wholesome, charitable views of men and things cannot be acquired by vegetating in one little corner of the earth all one's lifetime."* I felt like this was another great omen!

As we arrived at AK Sled Dog Tours, we saw row after row of boxes lined up symmetrically, along with a red line to which each husky was attached, so they had room to run.

I know it might not be the most humane setup, but the dogs were beautiful, well-mannered, and appeared happy, content, and filled with infectious adventure to pull the sleds. Many would sit on the top of these boxes, which were their homes, and survey the land around them, greeting the people who were coming to see them. I was surprised by the many color variations of the huskies. I expected them all to look like the black and white version that we normally see. Some were lighter colored, a mix of tan and white, and some were totally white. Others were darker brown, and of course the black and white ones. Some of them looked more like German Shepherds!

I got to steer my own sled along well-groomed trails in the forest, pulled by five huskies. My son steered his own sled as well, and my mom rode along with him. The guide led us, followed by my son in the middle, and I brought up the rear. It was a beautiful venture into the serene snow-bound forest that glittered in the morning sun. Crisp and cool and very refreshing. The air was so alive and fresh and was a joy to breathe in.

I felt one with my team of huskies as they pulled me along into the forest. They knew the way, and I surrendered to their knowing. The snow on either side of the trail was about a foot deep. The two lead dogs were darker, and the one on the left ran with his tail up while the one on the left ran with his tail down. They ran close together, side by side, occasionally nudging into each other as they ran. The dog in the middle was on the right side and had a darker coat, and also ran with its tail up. The two dogs that followed were a brown one on the right with his tail held straight out, and a white one on the left with its tail up. They stayed far apart from each other. Sometimes as we occasionally stopped to take in the beauty and give the dogs rest, they would eat the pristine snow. Enjoying family time amidst the wild, frozen, serene beauty of Alaska reminded me that even in the bitter cold, life is still worth living!

We came back home on March 23rd, and mom and I prepped for our road trip that would take us to Denver, where mom lives and where I'm from, and then all the way to Florida.

On March 25th, while we were loading up the truck, a beautiful green frog showed up in my yard and let me hold it. Another good sign to start the trip! We finished loading up the truck and got a good night's sleep. The next morning, we said our goodbyes to my son and his huskies and hit the road!

Flashback: November 2014

When Gary was diagnosed with throat cancer in November 2014, he was confident that he could heal himself again, just like he did with his back injury. While he made great strides in the first couple of years, the cancer came back in early 2017 with a vengeance. Nine months before Gary died, he reluctantly went in to have a feeding tube put in, as he couldn't swallow food and was rapidly losing weight, weighing in around 135 pounds on a 6-foot frame. He believed that this was a temporary fix, that it would just be to get nutrition into his body and get him strong again so that he could continue the fight. However, when we got to the ER, they would not put the feeding tube in unless they did a tracheostomy first because the tumor was closing in on his trachea, and they were surprised that he could breathe at all. He believed this was going to be temporary as well, that eventually, the trach would be removed once he was back on track with his health.

Alas, it was not to be. No miracle healing in the cards this time. As I reflect now, it's interesting to see the parallel of his thinking that the tracheostomy and the feeding tube could be temporary, just like the Harrington Rods were temporary. Yet, miracles happened in many other forms. Sometimes they come in ways you never expect. And that's the beauty of miracles!

What Are The Gifts?

Learning what repetitive, negative thinking can do to the body in the long term was one of the greatest things I learned from Gary's illness. When you're dealing with something like cancer, it usually is created by a long-term belief that usually stems from childhood. And whatever that belief is, and how that belief relates to the human body, is where illness will show up.

Over the course of our spiritual journey, we became familiar with Louise Hay's book, *You Can Heal Your Life*. Whenever we would have aches or pains, we would refer to that book and see what emotion was causing it. I didn't really take my physical pains very seriously until Gary got sick. Even then, I was so intent on taking care of Gary and keeping up with my work that I wasn't listening to my body's clues about what was going on with me. Even though I knew the power of thoughts and beliefs and how they affect the body, I wasn't taking care of myself. That's how I found myself, four months after Gary passed, in the hospital getting an emergency appendectomy. Emotionally, appendicitis indicates a fear of life and blocking the flow of good. I realized how I had created this illness by neglecting myself. And I remembered then, of course too late, the many cues that my body had been sending me over the past couple of years that I dismissed. The question I should have been asking was: *"What is this pain or disease trying to tell me?"*

When I made the decision to finally put myself first, that's when I really stepped into my knowingness and took the reins back. I started listening to my body. I took my power back.

Activity: Body Awareness

- What pain or tension are you carrying in your body right now?
- Where is it located in your body?
- What beliefs are supporting this pain or tension? A great reference is Louise Hay's book *You Can Heal Your Life* for emotions that are connected to body pain.

Gratitude, Laughter, Divine

Think about today, and answer these questions in your journal:

- What are you grateful for today?
- What made you laugh today?
- Did you feel the Divine today?

Chapter 4
Leg 2: Late March 2019

Gary Shares: "Forgiveness is when we recognize ourselves in others."

Not quite a month into leaving my job, I was still questioning my decision. As I was reading what I wrote in my journal after Gary died, I found this entry:

I want to decide what my future is, based on who my higher self is.

I want to tune in to my higher self, reconnect, listen to my higher voice, and take action based on that.

December 16, 2018

I spoke with my good friends yesterday; they helped me to get clear. I also found a meditation on connecting to my higher self. I did it before bed but fell asleep. I decided to do it again this morning to get all the way through. I did connect with my higher self! She wore a flowing ivory-colored dress that complimented her green eyes and beautiful long dark hair. She told me: "You are making the right choice. It's time for you. Bigger things are waiting for you. You deserve to be happy and free. You won't lose anything, and you are always loved."

On March 26th, we hit the road! Our goal for the entire trip was to take our time and stop whenever we had the desire to. We stopped at nearly every historical place of interest along the way. One interesting stop was Cascade Locks and Bonneville Dam in Oregon, where we learned about the fish ladders and how they managed the fisheries. Lewis and Clark camped near here on April 9, 1806. We saw fishing platforms built on the sides of river walls that were used by Native Americans. The landscape was so beautiful, with the rolling green hills amidst the mighty Columbia River. I found a beautiful gray feather that was another sign that Gary was nearby. I placed that feather on my dashboard as a constant reminder of why we were on this adventure.

We crossed the border into Idaho later that evening. We stayed in Boise, and the next morning found us in Bliss, Idaho, elevation 3265. I have a great selfie of mom and me in front of that Bliss sign, smiling and laughing! One memorable pullover was at the Malad Gorge State Park, one of Idaho's natural wonders. You can't even see anything as you're driving down I-84; no arresting landscape that would even hint at what is just beneath the highway bridge. We just happened to see the sign, and the word "gorge" intrigued us, so we pulled over. What we found was like a small version of the Grand Canyon, with a waterfall that plunged into the Devil's Washbowl. There were fissures in the ground along the trails that we walked, reminding us of the powerful geological energy that created this majestic area.

In Willard, Idaho, we stopped at a beautiful lake and encountered a heron, another sign of Gary's nearness. A heron had shown up for me and my two Dutch friends in Cancun, Mexico, the previous June, a few weeks after Gary passed. We were walking along the beach one evening close to midnight. I had some of Gary's ashes with me, as we had planned to spread them together in the ocean. We were debating on whether to wait until sunrise, and suddenly a heron landed in the surf near us. We decided that was our sign that this was the place to put his ashes. While we each took a small handful, the heron watched us and then flew away as we released his ashes into the sea. The next morning at sunrise, I walked alone along the beach and saw another heron nearby. I placed some more ashes in that spot. To this day, my friends and I often encounter herons, they in Holland and me wherever I happen to be. We delight in sending each other pictures to remind us that Gary is still around!

We stayed the night in Rock Springs, Wyoming, and the next day, we crossed over into Colorado. We stopped at my mom's house in Littleton for a couple days to rest, and then on March 30th, we hit the road again. We stopped in Cañon City to check out the prison there and got a great selfie of us next to the prison sign. We watched them bring in a new prisoner and felt like detectives trying to imagine what crime brought this person to prison! Was he a Red or Andy from *The Shawshank Redemption*? I sent him a prayer for a short stay and an escape to Zihuatanejo. Then this Thelma and Louise got back on the road! We stopped at the Royal Gorge and rode the gondola. It was a very windy day, and the ride was a bit unnerving, but the breathtaking beauty was worth it.

We arrived in Crestone, Colorado, and stayed in a nice Airbnb. We had heard that this was a highly energetic village at the foot of the western slope of the Sangre de Cristo Range, which in Spanish means the blood of Christ.

Crestone is a spiritual center where several world religions are represented.

The next day, we visited the Buddhist Jangchub Chorten Stupa of Enlightenment, where I learned more about what the stupa represents: Buddha's body, speech, and most especially, mind. It is a precise and powerful symbol of the Enlightened Mind and the path to its realization. I learned that the stupa symbolizes the five elements and their relationship to the enlightened mind. The base signifies earth and equanimity; the dome, water and indestructibility; the spire, fire and compassion; above the spire, wind and all-encompassing action; and at the very top, the jewel represents space and all-pervading awareness.

We hiked up a short path to a shrine where people left meaningful trinkets. There were Buddhist flags waving in the wind, and light snow was falling as we walked, making it a surreal moment in time.

We visited the Nada Carmelite Hermitage, part of the Spiritual Life Institute, which is a Roman Catholic Carmelite contemplative tradition. It was a beautiful and peaceful property reminiscent of Spanish adobe-style buildings. We spent some time in the chapel, which was simple and magical. A large cross was suspended above the pulpit with beautiful stained glass on either side, representing many cultures.

I found a beautiful two-toned heart-shaped rock while in Crestone, another sign from Gary!

March 31st brought us to La Jara, Colorado, where we stopped to honor a roadside memorial for Jeremy Richard Sisneros, just 25 years old. I left flower petals and said a prayer for his soul and his family. It had a "Please Ride Safely" sign with his name below. There was a tall and beautiful wooden cross with his name etched onto it down the vertical part and his date of birth and death on the horizontal part. A beautiful heart wreath hung on it, and to the left of it was another tall metal pole that had his first name spelled going down the pole with a heart on top. A heart wreath was hanging from that, and it was flanked by tall solar lights, which I'm sure were to keep the light on for his soul when the sun went down each evening.

One of the most profound experiences of this trip was honoring roadside memorials. We placed dried flowers on each site where we stopped. My purpose in doing this was to honor Gary's passing by honoring those that left this earth so traumatically and unexpectedly, in ways that didn't afford their families the opportunity to say goodbye. It reminded me how grateful I was to have been given time to say goodbye to Gary. Many of these memorials were so lovingly tended. We dwelt in the truth that every life has meaning and always provides lessons for everyone to expand and grow in Spirit.

In Conejos, Colorado, we stopped at a beautiful church, Nuestra Señora de Guadalupe, built in 1926. This simple yet beautiful church, Spanish for Our Lady of Guadalupe, celebrates the divine feminine.

All along our route through Colorado, we stopped anytime we saw a Denver and Rio Grande Western Railroad train. My mom retired from the railroad and began her career with her beloved D&RGW. I have many great photos of her smiling happily with "her trains!"

We ended the month of March in New Mexico, the Land of Enchantment, where we synchronistically saw a sign for Ojo Caliente, where Gary had stopped on his healing road trip after his back injury! It was snowing as we toured the spa and had lunch. I bought a rock that had the symbol of the resort, which was a circle within a circle within another circle, as I knew Gary would have bought it for me!

On our way out, we stopped on a steep hill at another roadside memorial for Joseph Broyles, 35, with a white cross and red roses. And then another one for Fabian Lawrence Mata, with a bright blue wreath with a photo of a young, beautiful woman in sunglasses, her hair slicked back in a ponytail. There were crosses, angels, and solar lights around her name stenciled on stones and surrounded by more beautiful rocks. I bet it looked beautiful when the sun went down.

We ended the day and the month in Truth or Consequences, New Mexico, which was named after the famous radio show. It was originally called Hot Springs and changed its name to win the contest by the radio show for its ten-year anniversary, which was to air in the first town that changed its name to Truth or Consequences.

We stayed at the Sierra Grande Resort and Spa, which rests on mineral-enriched geothermal hot springs. They offered private indoor and outdoor hot springs that honor the legendary healing traditions first established by the region's Native Americans. It was beautifully decorated in the Southwestern tradition, and we gratefully drifted off to sleep, dreaming about our spa experience to come in the morning.

Flashback: December 2014-May 2015

Because of the severity of the cancer, we knew that we had to do something right away. The doctor who diagnosed him said that without any intervention at all, he had six months to live. She, of course, recommended the usual treatment, which was the removal of the cancer, which could include part of the tongue where they believed the cancer originated, along with anything else that might need to be removed, followed by chemotherapy and radiation. Gary did not want to have any kind of surgery, and he especially didn't want chemotherapy.

After doing some research, we found a place in Los Angeles that was doing a combination of low-dose radiation and hyperthermia, which is a high-heat treatment. They'd had good success with many kinds of cancers, including head and neck cancer, which can be the most difficult to treat. We made the decision to move Gary to Los Angeles so that he could begin treatment. This was a difficult decision to make because I still had to work in Washington to pay for the insurance and the cost to live in Los Angeles. It was challenging to get insurance in place, as we hadn't had any health insurance at that point. Once we finally got him on a plan, it was already mid-January.

We packed up Gary's truck, and he drove to Los Angeles. He got settled into a small apartment that he called the dark hole. It was exceedingly small, dreary, and not much fun to be in. I felt so guilty not being there with him every day during his treatments. He told me from the beginning that he would be fine by himself. Just like when he broke his back, he wanted to have a single-minded focus to heal without the fears and judgments from well-meaning family and friends.

For four months, from mid-January until mid-May, Monday through Friday, with a few breaks, he endured daily targeted radiation and heat therapy. Over the course of the treatment, he rapidly lost his taste buds, and his salivary glands stopped working. He continued to lose weight and gained a host of other severe reactions that greatly affected his quality of life. I visited him every month for long weekends. It was so hard to see him, as it was glaringly apparent how much his body had been affected by the treatment.

The highlight was in February when I brought our Seahawks gear to watch Seattle play the New England Patriots in the Super Bowl. We found space at a Mexican restaurant and bar near Venice Beach where we could watch the game. We ordered mega margaritas and got totally hammered. I missed the half time show with Katy Perry along with most of the second half. According to Gary, I was having fun. I just have no memory of it! However, I do remember how the game finished because it was so disappointing, with our Seahawks on the losing end. We stumbled out of the bar with a big bar tab. Apparently, I bought several rounds for our new friends, and neither of us remembers driving home. Gary joked that he was the designated drunk driver that night. Someone was watching over us and made sure we made it home safely! (Note: I don't encourage drinking and driving, we were very irresponsible!)

What Are The Gifts?

We take for granted how seamlessly our body works for us. When Gary could no longer taste his food or have the benefit of saliva in his mouth, it made me aware of how beautifully designed the human body is. How the simple things that we enjoy, we take for granted and don't fully enjoy in the present moment. Simple things like eating a chocolate croissant, drinking a great cup of coffee, eating

Thai or any spicy food. Drinking a glass of red wine or downing a shot of tequila. Being able to easily swallow the food we eat with the help of our saliva.

These were Gary's favorite things that he could no longer enjoy. Many times, when we would be out eating, I was his "taster," explaining to him what it tasted and felt like for me so that he could imagine it in his mind and override what he wasn't experiencing. Now, traveling the world without him, I make a conscious effort to really taste what I'm eating, whether it's sweet, salty, savory, or spicy, to really enjoy the texture, and to feel my mouth watering at the thought or sight of amazing food or drink.

Activity: Who Inspires You?

- Who do you look up to? Find two people, it could be famous people, inspiring people, historical figures.
- Google them and learn more about their life and accomplishments.
- What traits do they have? List at least five. Do you have any of these traits?
- Why do you admire them?
- How can you emulate them in your life?

Gratitude, Laughter, Divine

Think about today, and answer these questions in your journal:

- What are you grateful for today?
- What made you laugh today?
- Did you feel the Divine today?

Chapter 5
Leg 3: April 2019

Gary Shares: "It's time for me to step forward and share my light for all."

We woke up on the first day of April to clear skies and beautiful weather in Truth or Consequences. After a simple breakfast in the hotel restaurant, we went to our private spa room. Entering, we walked down a few steps to a large spa with seats around the side. The entire room, which was the size of a large master bath, was tiled throughout. The mineral spring water was nice and warm and so soothing. We thoroughly enjoyed our session, and when our hour was up, we reluctantly put on our plush spa robes and slippers and made our way back to our room. Our minds were still in the haziness of an amazing soak. We turned right instead of left at the top of the stairs and attempted to open the door of the wrong room with our old-fashioned skeleton key. And it worked! To my mom's shock and to the dismay of the person in the room, we realized our mistake! With profuse apologies, we made a quick retreat to our room down the hall.

Once we got our wits together, we dressed, packed up, and checked out. Before we left, we spent some time enjoying the tranquil grounds of this beautiful property. There was a medicine wheel in the front gardens of the hotel, along with a few places to sit in the shade of the wispy palm trees. We made our way to the back of the hotel and took a nice stroll in the terraced gardens with beautiful metal sculptures among the rocks. Cactus was everywhere, and many were just beginning to open their flower buds. Seeing vibrant flowers on a prickly cactus is one of the most breathtaking contrasts. When we reached the top of the gardens, we witnessed a beautiful view of the surrounding mountains below bright blue skies.

We hit the road and bade goodbye to the Land of Enchantment at high noon, just like an old western movie! And at 12:01 p.m., we crossed the state line into Texas, greeted by the welcome sign that said, *Drive Friendly—the Texas Way.*

We arrived in Fort Stockton around mid-evening. We stopped at a rest area to refresh ourselves and to take a little walk to stretch our tired bodies. Along the way, we found many beautiful flowers. There was a huge plant like aloe. It had large stalks that looked like they had just burst forth with beautiful big white flowers and new buds that were magnificent among the spiky fronds of the plant. We came upon a small ground covering with delicate purple flowers, each with five heart-shaped petals, in various shades of purple, among beautiful deep green leaves, spreading out over the dusty, dry, cracked, rocky ground. There were beautiful orange flowers that looked like poppies but much lower to the ground with beautiful yellow centers.

Another plant had a flower-shaped twisted rope about 12 inches long. They stood tall and erect among green furry leaves, and I can only imagine that once all the little petals within that long stem bloomed, it would be amazingly beautiful. Next to that was another long-stemmed flower that

46

had delicate white flowers with a touch of red in the center. Each sturdy furry-looking stem had between 15 and 20 little flowers on the top half. The effect was of one long and beautiful fairy wand. And the grand finale: a beautiful bright yellow morning glory which reminded me of the flowers my grandmother grew in her garden. It was a truly magnificent display of nature, and in a rest stop to boot! Beauty abounds everywhere! We tumbled back into the truck and made our way to Ozona, Texas, for the night.

The next morning, we hit the road under a beautiful light blue sky with a sliver of a moon showing us the way. We arrived in San Antonio and drove straight to the Riverwalk, one of my favorite places in the world. I had come here as a teenager on a family summer trip, one of our last trips before my parents divorced. I remembered a magical time coming to life in my mind, of strolling through all the twists and turns and riding on the riverboats. I loved being there again. Mom and I enjoyed a river cruise and reveled in the beauty of the Riverwalk. As we rode under a bridge, we saw the locks of love on the fence of the bridge, reminding me of a similar sight in Italy years before with Gary. My mom's name is Rita, and there were four little shops and restaurants that had her name, and I got a picture of her underneath each one: Mercado Rita's, Bonita Rita's, Pizzarita's, and Rita's On the River Margarita Bar!

The next morning, we arrived in Port Allen, Louisiana, near Baton Rouge. We crossed the Horace Wilkinson Bridge, an amazing steel cantilever bridge that holds the distinction of being the highest bridge on the Mississippi River. By midafternoon we drove through the Pearl River

Wildlife Management Center on the Louisiana side and crossed over the Pearl River into Mississippi.

As we continued, we came upon Pass Christian, where we spent about an hour on this beautiful white sandy beach! We enjoyed nature's airshow as several groups of sea birds flew in formation, from four in one group to six in another, skimming the top of the water with the precision of fighter jets. Pelicans were diving like kamikazes, one right after another. Most of them gracefully, except for one. He attempted the dive too close to the water and didn't have time to get his wings in place. It was quite the pelican belly flop!

We soaked in the beauty as the gentle waves rolled in and out, under a beautiful blue sky with swaths of clouds draped across. As is my custom, actually Gary's and mine, I collected treasures from the sand: seashells with intricate patterns worn into them, a sea nut, and an interesting bone that looked like a spine. The sand was so soft, like fine sugar and perfect for walking barefoot.

We reluctantly got back on the road and took Highway 90 along the coast through Biloxi, across the Biloxi Bay, and found our way onto Highway 10. Two hours later, in the early evening, we arrived at Polecat Bay in Mobile, Alabama. As we crossed the Tensaw River, we saw a Navy ship docked there.

Finally arriving in Florida, we crossed into Pensacola, to the neon *Florida Welcomes You* sign, bright as the sun, welcoming us to the Sunshine State. We still had another five hours to go and arrived in Jacksonville in the early morning hours of April 4th.

We spent two days in Jacksonville, recovering from the long trip and enjoying the company of my daughter and her English springer spaniel, Chewie. Then, bright and early on a Saturday morning, we drove to Fort Lauderdale to embark on a cruise workshop, Magical Voyage of the Soul, with John Holland and Colette Baron-Reid. We would meet many wonderful men and women, all striving for a better life and thriving in the connection of the group.

We checked into our cruise with the Holland America Line in the early afternoon. A huge hummingbird painted on the port building was a great sign to send us off! We found our room, which, although small with two twin beds and a small sofa, had a small balcony. Having been on cruises before with only a porthole window, this was truly a luxury! I spent many a morning and evening watching the sunrise and set over the beautiful Atlantic Ocean on our private balcony.

At 4:47 p.m., we set sail. It was a beautiful sunny day on the Stranahan River, with a slight breeze as we left the dock amidst celebratory music playing over the loudspeakers of the ship. We sailed into a spectacular sunset at sea, with shades of yellow, orange, and gold, amidst a few gray clouds.

We had many amazing spiritual experiences during the workshop while listening and learning from these two wonderful teachers. It was a great reminder of how powerful we are, whether alive or in spirit. During one of Colette's mediumship sessions, she said that there were two dogs appearing to her, black and white, medium-sized. She also mentioned that there was a gentleman whose name started with a B. I remember saying to my mom that Brad (my late ex-husband) had an English springer spaniel that had died, but I didn't know who the second dog would be. My daughter currently had an English springer spaniel, so I dismissed that this was for me since her dog was still alive.

Earlier, Colette had taken us through a forgiveness mediation, where she guided us along a sandy beach to a white temple. Inside the temple would be someone with whom we needed to connect. I assumed I would see Gary, as I felt I needed forgiveness for the shortcomings I believed I demonstrated as his caregiver. To my surprise, my late ex-husband Brad was in the temple! I didn't receive any communication from him, just a feeling of shock.

The next day, I had a spa appointment at 7:00 p.m. I received a call in the early evening saying they had a 6:00 p.m. slot open. I headed down, and as I arrived, Colette was there scheduling her spa appointment. We were already acquainted as she was a colleague of my former employer. She stopped to say hello, and I shared with her about my meditation experience and that I thought the man with the two dogs might be my ex-husband but dismissed it because the second English springer spaniel was alive. She said she sometimes sees people and animals who are still alive, and she asked what my ex-husband's name was. When I told her it was Brad, she said, "Remember, I said it starts with a Br, like Brad or something." I didn't remember hearing that because I had already determined it was not for me because of the dog discrepancy. She was confident it was him.

At the next workshop session, she pointed to me and said she had a message from Brad. He was asking for my forgiveness, that I was a great wife and mother, and he didn't treat me as I deserved. She also shared details about his death that she could not have known. My mom was in tears as I sat in shock, hearing this. I realized that was why he appeared in the temple. After we returned to Jacksonville while sharing this story with my daughter, I learned that Brad did, in fact, have *two* English springer spaniels that had passed. I immediately connected with Colette to let her know that she was spot on!

While I was reading through my journals in preparation for writing this book, I came across notes from a private reading that I had with John Holland in January 2019. In this reading, my late grandfather (who also died from throat cancer and whom Gary never met) brought Gary through. Gary shared many things with John that only Gary and I would know. I'll share a few highlights here: that I had just placed a family photo on the fireplace mantel; he asked John to ask about my rings, which days before, I had taken several Gary had given me to a jeweler to combine into one ring. Gary's late mother came through and had John ask me about life insurance. We had learned a few months before Gary died that he had a small life insurance policy through his former employer that we weren't aware of. These and many others confirmed that it was indeed Gary coming through. To my surprise, I had made a note about two dogs that John saw. That didn't make sense to me at the time of the reading, and John said to write it down because later it might make sense. I believe the two dogs that John saw in January were the same two dogs that Colette saw in April. How synchronistic that I got to be at a workshop with both! The

Universe is always sending us information, and sometimes it takes many experiences and people to get through to us!

The following morning, we docked at Key West. I love the Florida Keys and was excited to be here again. Everywhere we walked in Key West, bougainvillea abounded in many shades of pink, orange, red, and purple, growing along white picket fences.

Our first stop was to take a tour of the Harry S. Truman Little White House Museum. The home was a stately two-story, miniature White House with American flag banners hanging below each window on the upper floor. The gardens and lawn were gorgeous and surrounded by a dark green wrought iron fence. Inside, the house was decorated in the style of the times. President Truman visited eleven times from November 1946 to March 1952. Looking at the log of his first visit, it was interesting to learn how many people accompanied him: nine high-level guests, sixteen staff members, and thirteen secret service agents, along with the White House Press Association, which included fifteen newspaper correspondents, four radio personnel, four photographers, and five in the motion picture pool. Quite an entourage of sixty-seven people, including the President!

Our second visit was to the Ernest Hemingway Home at 907 Whitehead Street, a gorgeous haven surrounded by a red brick wall. As we made our way through the entrance flanked by huge palm trees, we came upon the two-story yellow house with arched windows and doors with black wrought iron railings on the second level. There were beautiful gardens around the house with many places to sit and enjoy the scenery. The famous Hemingway cats were everywhere and included about 40-50, half of which were polydactyl (six-toed) cats. There was even a small cat cemetery in the garden. Hemingway named all his cats after famous people, a tradition that continues to this day. Some of the cats roaming the grounds during our visit were Rita Hayworth, Ginger Rogers, Jackie O, and Olivia De Havilland. Daisy Buchanan napped between two pillows on the white chenille bedspread on Hemingway's ornate wooden bed.

Hemingway's studio was behind the main house, with a shaker front on the second story. It had a twelve-paned window flanked by bright yellow shutters and green trim. There were cats hanging out on the roof as if they were waiting for Hemingway himself to enter. Fortunately, it was not a hot tin roof (a nod to another Key West writer)! We climbed the steep stairway, holding onto the wrought iron railing leading up to the studio. The studio was quite the cozy man-cave, with an antelope mounted above the built-in bookcase that spanned the wall between two French doors. A dark wooden writing-table was in the center of the room, where an old-fashioned typewriter sat as if patiently waiting for the celebrated author to plop down and spin another tale.

Two days later found us disembarking on Grand Turk, into beautiful turquoise waters under brilliant blue skies and a myriad of puffy clouds. We hopped on a tour bus and spent the next hour learning about this beautiful country. We passed by a replica of the space shuttle capsule in which John Glenn rode in February 1962. His connection to Grand Turk began on February 20th, as part of the Mercury project and space capsule Friendship 7. Glenn landed in nearby waters after his historic orbit of Earth. He was the first American to orbit Earth, circling the globe three times in four hours and fifty-six minutes. After his splashdown, he was brought to Grand Turk for his debriefing and medical exam. The capsule joined him later when it was delivered by ship.

During our tour, we encountered many wild and very friendly donkeys. Starting in the 1700s, Bermudians arrived on the island seasonally to rake salt from the salt ponds. They used donkeys to pull loaded carts from the evaporation ponds to the piers where the salt was loaded onto ships. During the offseason, the donkeys were free to roam, which created a huge population of wild donkeys. The highlight for us was a sweet momma and her baby donkey, nursing near the historic 1852 lighthouse.

As we walked back to the tour bus, we stopped at the Mary Prince Monument. It was a cream-colored wall that had an arched shape at the top, with the words *"To be free is very sweet,"* with a notation saying, *"Mary Prince, years before her freedom, speaking to her owner."* I was intrigued by the photo I took and decided to learn more about her. Mary was a black West Indian woman who spent ten years in the Grand Turk salt ponds, toiling in the harsh conditions of the salt industry, from approximately 1802–1812. The full quote is: *"All slaves want to be free – to be free is very sweet."*

The *History of Mary Prince, A West-Indian Slave,* was written by her and published in 1831 by London's Anti-Slavery Society. Her writings provide rich details about the various aspects of enslavement she experienced. Prince is the earliest known freed slave to author such a testimony. She was born in 1788 in Bermuda, had five owners, and was enslaved in three British Overseas Territories – Bermuda, Grand Turk Island, and Antigua – before being freed in London in 1828.

Grand Turk has hectares of salt ponds, where slaves once raked salt into large heaps ready for shipment. Today, the salt ponds serve as bird sanctuaries on the island. Canals connecting the ocean to these ponds are still obvious, and slave-owner residences and slave dwellings still stand. Prince was one of the thousands of slaves forced to build the ponds, maintain them, and labor in them for their Bermudian slave-owners for up to 17 hours a day.

'I was given a half barrel and a shovel,' she said in her book, 'and had to stand up to my knees in the water, from four o'clock in the morning till nine, when we were given some Indian corn boiled in water, which we were obliged to swallow as fast as we could for fear the rain would come on and melt the salt. We worked through the heat of the day; the sun flaming upon our heads like fire and raising salt blisters in those parts which were not completely covered.'

I was grateful to have learned about Mary Prince, especially considering the current racial tensions of 2020. I was also especially humbled and grateful for the gift of those who ventured before us. Their stories remind us of the power we use incorrectly when people are treated like property rather than extolled as unique and powerful human beings in their own right.

After the tour, the bus left us at the beach, where we spent time relaxing by the turquoise waters under an umbrella. We walked along the white sandy beach and came upon a rocky beach with big rocks, where we walked and cooled off in the pools. The sound of the waves crashing over the rocks was a great soundtrack for the sailboat anchored in the distance. We found more sea treasures, so many varieties of shells and cloudy white sea glass. My favorite find was a seashell like the one the Goddess Venus is always shown standing in. As we returned to the boat and then set sail for the open sea, we were mesmerized by the beauty of Grand Turk, where the many shades of turquoise water were like nothing I've ever seen.

The next day we sailed into San Felipe de Puerto Plata in the Dominican Republic. We strolled across the long gangway onto the island, got our colored wrist bands, and waited in the market center for our tour to start. When our group was called, we proceeded through a long, covered walkway where we were greeted by the sign *"Welcome to the Amber Coast."* We were serenaded by a trio of musicians wearing bright green island shirts, black pants, and straw hats in different styles. The first musician was playing a long tin can that he beat with a spoon as he danced and grooved. The second musician was sitting on a chair playing a double-sided bongo drum, using his hand on the left side and a drumstick on the right. The third musician was playing his heart out on his golden saxophone.

We hopped on a tour bus for the thirty-minute ride to a cacao factory, Asoprocon, run by local women. This was a volunteer tourism excursion where we planted cacao seeds and learned about how they are grown and harvested. Our next task was in the production area. Here, we were warmly greeted by the women with a song and dance. The women ranged from young teenagers to grandmothers, all incredibly happy, young at heart, and full of love. It was so inspiring, witnessing the love they had for each other and their community. We had to wear white hair coverings while sorting out the cacao seeds, which were laid out on small trays. Any that were broken or not to standard were discarded. Mom and I had a good laugh that we looked like Lucy and Ethel working in the chocolate factory, trying to keep up!

We then went to the packaging station, where we bagged up single chocolate pieces into packages of ten, inserted cards, and sealed them. Next, we got to make the individual pieces by ladling the chocolate into the shaped candy molds. When our shift was complete, we enjoyed some bread and a cup of hot and spicy cacao.

When we got back to the market center, we stopped at a baseball memorial honoring Major League Baseball players. I learned that since the 1950s, more than four hundred Dominicans have played in the major leagues, including superstars Pedro Martinez, Sammy Sosa, Alex Rodriguez, Bartolo Colon, David Ortiz, and Albert Pujols. Dominicans love baseball, and for more than 100 years, the sport has been at the center of their cultural life. The country supplies more players to major league baseball than any other besides the United States. Thirty percent of players in the major leagues are foreign-born, and most of those are from the Dominican Republic.

Back on the high seas, we witnessed a beautiful sunrise on the North Atlantic! Hues of pink, orange, and yellow were painted over the horizon with clouds floating above. After all the excursions of the past couple of days, we had a day at sea to chill, relax, and enjoy a full day at our workshop.

During the workshop, I drew two oracle cards: Coming to Life and Flying. I'm always amazed at how accurate oracle cards can be. As I've since learned, oracle cards are not about predicting the future. They are about providing divine direction to navigate our path to our divine purpose. As I reflected on the many changes I had made in the past few months, I did indeed feel like I was coming to life and flying into my new me!

The next morning brought us to the beautiful indigo waters of the Bahamas. We docked at Half Moon Cay, which was a private beach owned by the cruise line. Our excursion for this stop was a boat ride and snorkeling around a sunken ship. I ventured off the boat with about twelve other snorkelers and swam into the tranquil warm, turquoise waters. Snorkeling is a challenge for me, but once I got the rhythm of it and surrendered my fears to Neptune, I was ushered into a fantastic underwater world. All around the shipwreck were so many colorful fish and beautiful bright purple sea fans. The corroded bland metal of the ship was a stark contrast to all the vibrant colors that splashed before my eyes. So many times, I have allowed my fears to stop me from experiencing life. I am so glad that I stepped past my fear of not being able to breathe and allowed the embrace of this magnificent underwater world.

My mom stayed on the boat and got some great photos and videos of me. The video of me swimming out was so cute. I looked back at my mom and waved nervously, just like a little girl would do! And then a fun photo of me coming back to the boat, goggles on my forehead and snorkel to the side, with a big grin on my face, proud of my accomplishment. I love having these photos and videos to look back on as proof of my bravery, for the days when I question if I have any courage left, and for the days when I just need to be reminded of how grateful I am for this life.

Back at the beach, we had one hour to relax. As we walked along the white sandy beach, I found a heart seashell and knew that Gary was near and proud of my courage! We found a couple beach loungers and took in the beauty, me with my heart shell by my feet and mom with her cute Dominican sun hat. As we walked off the beach on our way back to the dock, we passed a sign that said, *"I wish I could stay here forever,"* and I concurred!

Each evening on the cruise, as we returned to our room, we were greeted by fun googly-eyed towel animals created by our wonderful housekeeping staff; a pig, an orangutan, hanging from our ceiling, a beautiful swan, an elephant, and one that was a mystery, perhaps a crab, a shrimp, or a dragonfly. One of the things I love about cruises is how the staff makes sure your every need is met! I surely needed to feel pampered and loved and was totally showered with great care.

We returned to my daughter's in Jacksonville, and on April 15th, we celebrated Chewie's third birthday. My daughter got him a frozen doggie cupcake with white frosting and sprinkles around the sides with three long candles. Chewie wasn't too excited about the candles, and he ran away and hid on the couch. My daughter blew them out for him after we sang Happy Birthday. Then he was happy to gobble up the treat on the patio where he made quite a mess. Of course, we didn't have to clean up after him, because he cleaned everything up on his own!

One of the things that helped me to stay present and feel happiness every day was taking Chewie on daily walks. These walks allowed me to watch how he enjoyed every moment of the walk and witness his curiosity about everything he passed. He taught me to appreciate all the lizards and geckos that constantly dart across the sidewalks and hop across the grass, as he occasionally tried to catch one. Fortunately, he never did. He showed me that it's okay to get excited to see people or other animals and realize that most times, they appreciate being stopped for a sniff and a hello. He helped me to be more open to smiling at and talking to perfect strangers with their dogs. I've never been much of a dog person, but between my son's huskies and my daughter's English springer spaniel, I'm slowly becoming one! I do love my cat, Gizmo, an outdoor cat that we finally allowed inside once Gary passed (he was allergic). I love having animals around. They are amazing to help us move through our grief.

During our stay in Florida, we took a day trip to St Augustine. We visited the Fountain of Youth Archaeological Park, where Ponce de Leon discovered the magical elixir in

1513. I had the opportunity to take a drink, a quick sulphury swallow, and I must say I didn't feel much younger! We roamed through the village, visiting a simple church and thatched huts. We enjoyed the cannon demonstration by swashbuckling pirates and marveled at the many beautiful peacocks roaming among us, expressing their voices in their unique, somewhat annoying way!

As we walked onto the Matanzas River Sanctuary, I was thinking about Gary. I read the signs about which animals were native to this area. I saw there were turtles, and I had these thoughts run through my mind: 1. Gary loved turtles; 2. An image of the alpaca blanket with a turtle design that I bought him for his last Christmas; and 3. It would be nice to see a turtle. As I walked further down the boardwalk, a turtle swam up close to me. It was about a foot in length and swam around for several minutes while I videoed!

We lost track of time and missed the last tour bus back to our car. I guess we enjoyed ourselves like children and entered that "no-time" dimension, perhaps compliments from that sulfur sip at the fountain of youth we had earlier? It's a good thing that "this time" has Ubers!

Later, we decided to make the three-hour drive to Tampa to visit our cousins. On the way, in Wesley Chapel, a beautiful yellow dragonfly appeared inside the truck on my driver's side door below the window. It was almost like magic that he was there. We had been on the road for hours, and you think we would have noticed a dragonfly! It stayed on my side of the window for several minutes and then flew over to my mom's side to hang out with her. We drove with it for about 15 minutes, then pulled over and let it out! No idea how it got in! Hi Gary!

Flashback: November 2015

Even with Gary's salivary glands and taste buds severely diminished, we were able to continue as usual, and he often traveled with me. At the end of November 2015, we were in Spain for a work trip and extended it another week to have some fun vacation time together. Wonderful friends who lived in Mallorca offered us their guest house. We spent four days there, and it was one of the best vacations we had together. It was certainly a celebratory time after Gary had completed his treatment and moved back home. He was doing so much better and was starting to gain weight. Although his salivary glands never fully recovered, he was starting to regain some of his taste buds, which was great because Gary was a total foodie and loved drinking red wine. We had a magical time driving around the island of Mallorca. We found great restaurants and enjoyed the yummy cuisine. We explored beautiful coves where we were able to swim and float while enjoying the clear turquoise waters under the brilliant blue skies. We enjoyed going to the village square of our little town to have coffee or dinner, or just sit outside enjoying the beauty and simplicity of this sweet European village.

I have a beautiful photo taken of Gary while we were climbing up into an old stone tower that overlooked the sea. It had a beautiful arched doorway, and as he was climbing up the ladder, the light flooding in illuminated him brilliantly. I felt sure that this was a sign that we were well on our way past the cancer and back to the healthy and vibrant Gary of my dreams. Everywhere we went on this island, there were beautiful doors: ornate, simple, artistic, weathered, and colorful. It felt like we were being shown doors to infinite possibilities for an exciting new future.

What Are The Gifts?

My favorite memory from the Mallorca trip is of Gary lightly holding me up with his hand on my lower back as I floated in the warm turquoise waters. Every time I would flail about, he would gently tell me that I was safe, to just relax and let him support me. After a few attempts, I finally let go and just allowed myself to float. The feeling of being safe was so profound.

Whenever I feel unsafe or scared, I remember this moment. I remember that Gary is always with me, supporting and loving me, just like when he was here. I remember that Spirit always has my back and loves me unconditionally. More importantly, I remember that I'm in control of my life, and I have everything I need within to create joy and happiness. Yes, even without Gary.

Activity: Transformation Through Travel

- If you could travel anywhere, where would you go? Why?
- What do you want to experience there?
- Google that country and list ten things that you would do when you get there. Plan it!
- If you have no desire to travel, then plan an adventure in your own city.

Gratitude, Laughter, Divine

Think about today, and answer these questions in your journal:

- What are you grateful for today?
- What made you laugh today?
- Did you feel the Divine today?

Chapter 6
Leg 4: May 2019

Gary Shares: "I now experience a harmonious balance of mind, body, spirit."

As the new month of May arrived, my old doubts began to creep back in. I was enfolded in my loving family, yet constantly reminded of what I was missing. Watching younger couples basking in the newness of their love and connection reminded me of what I once had with Gary. Seeing older couples enjoy their time together, holding hands, laughing, and smiling reminded me of what I didn't have. All of this made me envious and angry. Why did this happen to me? Life is so unfair. I know that everything happens for a reason, but couldn't I have been given the grace of a few more years? Years to explore retirement and adventure together? At the very least, couldn't Gary's illness have been less horrific?

As I silently grieved within, we drove to Clearwater Beach. Strolling through a park, we came upon a statue of Theodoros Griego. It was dated April 14, 1528, and stated that he was the first Greek in America. Four hundred and ninety-one years ago, another soul began his new journey in a foreign land with hopes of creating a new life. I sent a silent prayer of gratitude for the reminder that every one of us comes into this life on a journey, and we must allow our curiosity to keep charting new territory for us.

We walked out onto the pier, and a pure white heron greeted me; I'm sure a hello from Gary. Another one was walking around, a bit tousled and creamy colored. A third one was a little more nicely groomed, with feathers in many shades of gray. He enjoyed the company of a pelican, sitting next to him on the railing. There were many friendly pelicans on the pier. It was a bit frightening to be so close to them, as they look so prehistoric. My favorite had a brown mohawk down the back of his head and neck, fluffy and spikey like a young rebel. It's amazing to see how they fold up their wings so compactly. When they are outstretched, the wingspan is enormous.

A few days later, mom and I were back on the road. We took a different route back to see new terrain. We arrived in Atlanta, Georgia, and found a sign for the Gone with the Wind Museum, a favorite movie of ours. As a little girl, I got to see it with my parents when the movie was re-released in the theaters. I had warts treated on my left knee earlier that day and had a bandage covering it. Mom was afraid that Grandpa would attempt his own wart removal and took me with her, leaving my siblings behind. What a treasured memory for me! My daughter is named after Melanie Wilkes, the gentle, kind, and beautiful rival of Scarlet. I have fun pictures of mom and me hugging a life-size Rhett Butler and Scarlet O'Hara.

Later, we crossed into Jasper, Tennessee. The sign said: *Welcome to the Soundtrack of America, Made in Tennessee.* We stayed in Nashville that evening, and the next morning we hopped on a tour bus. We drove past the Jack Daniels Building, Victory Park, the Bicentennial Capitol Mall State Park, and an impressive replica of the Parthenon. We enjoyed the sights as we went down Music Row: Southern Ground Studios, the RCA Victor Recording Studio, and a fun statue with naked men and women dancing around each other. On Broadway was the famous Legends Corner bar that had a huge mural with Dolly Parton, Reba McIntyre, Taylor Swift, Blake Shelton, Johnny Cash, and many other famous country superstars.

A few hours later, we arrived in Kentucky to a plain welcome center sign, *Kentucky Unbridled Spirit*. The next sign we saw was *Missouri Welcomes You*, as we later crossed the impressive Stan Musial Veterans Memorial Bridge into Saint Louis. We stopped to see the Gateway Arch, which was closed due to flooding. Nearby, there were statues barely showing their heads above the rushing water: a visual reminder not to flood myself with negative thoughts or too many distractions. We arrived at Unity Village later in the evening to do a site visit for a future event.

We awoke the next morning and found a pancake machine! You just push a button, and your pancake magically appears! I must get one of these, my non-cook voice stated! After breakfast, we ventured onto the gorgeous grounds. Around the tall watchtower was a Prayer Garden, with twelve prayer patios, each with its own power sculpture. The meditative prayer walk began at Understanding, and continued through Will, Imagination, Faith, Zeal, Power, Love, Wisdom, Strength, Order, Life, and finally Release. These powers are also in the walls around the entryway into the main chapel. As I made my way around the circle, I came upon a sign that said: *Everything will change when your desire to move on exceeds your desire to hold on.* (Alan H. Cohen).

I asked myself, am I ready to move on? The question was still to be answered. I feared what moving on would mean. What would it say about me as a person, and what would others think? Why did I care so much about what others thought? That's a great question. I felt intuitively that if I could answer that question and move past the fear, my new life would be much easier to create and then begin to live.

We then came upon the labyrinth, where we walked around the circle, following it around and around, left and right, up and down, until we got to the center. Then we made our way back out again. The purpose of meandering through the labyrinth, in a way that initially seems unproductive, is actually an exercise in being mindful and present as you make your way through. You become aware of what you are thinking and feeling, and the physical process of wandering reminds us of what goes on in our minds if left unchecked. The gift of the labyrinth is to gain control of our presence so that we can do the same when we get back to our reality.

As I walked through, I realized that my grief was exactly like the labyrinth. Until I was able to gain control of my wandering and angry mind, I would never find my center. Upon gaining control of my thoughts and finding my center, I could get clear on who I really am and then begin making my way out. I would surely still meander, but the key was that I was now aware. In this newfound awareness, my wandering towards my new life would become more purposeful!

Refreshed in mindset, I went to check out the Nature Trail, where the sign happily told me: *There's a wonderful adventure ahead of you!* The trail took me under a railroad bridge with some positive graffiti, the best being "shine brighter than before" and "teach peace." I crossed over a fast-flowing river, whose sound was loud yet soothing. The river was a bit high, so it was challenging to cross some of the foot bridges. The trail led me to a beautiful lake where there were large birds swimming peacefully. On the way back, I met a beautiful red cardinal, a sign that this was a great place for an event.

We finally made it to *Colorful Colorado* later that evening. We were back in Denver before Mother's Day, as we had promised to deliver flowers for my sister's floral shop in the Highlands. It was a wonderful experience meeting so many beautiful mommas! One older lady was so excited to receive flowers and continued waving as I drove off. I got the sense that while she loved the flowers, she really craved connection. It's always lovely to get flowers, yet the simple act of connection is so much more appreciated.

I left an offering of flower petals at a memorial near my sister's shop. A white bike was attached to a street sign with colorful flowers in the spokes and white tulips in the basket. The sign said *In Memoriam: Dave Martinez.* He was struck by a hit and run driver in December 2018 near this intersection while riding home from work. On January 7, 2019, he died due to injuries sustained in the crash. I said a silent prayer for him and his family.

May was ending as I flew back home to Washington State. A few days later, my son and I went to Oregon for a family wedding. It was the first time we had seen Gary's family since his death nearly a year earlier. They had a lovely In Memoriam Table. *We know you'd be here today if Heaven weren't so far away*, with pictures of their grandparents and Uncle Gary. A great picture of him on one of our Mexico trips, when he was looking so healthy and happy, was a bittersweet reminder of loss. Yet, it was soothed by the beautiful connection of young love. New love is an example that life is ever-renewing, a great reminder of beginnings and endings and all the beautiful memories that we create in between.

We returned home to Washington to be greeted by an offering from our cat, Gizmo. On my new Hello welcome mat, we found various rodent parts! I guess he wanted to make sure we had something to eat after a long day of travel! I became nervous about how I would endure being in our home where Gary had passed a year earlier. I worried about the constant reminder every morning that this was my new reality. Surprisingly, I really enjoyed being in the energy of love that we had created over so many years.

I thought about all the signs on this leg of the journey that were showing me the beauty and mystery of life. That we all have allies, whether it be family, new friends met along the way, nature's creatures, or Mother Nature's infinite beauty.

As if to calm my fears, I had a visit from a beautiful red-throated hummingbird. Gary, and his voice! What a great way to end the month, being reminded of the power of my voice!

Flashback: February 2016

In February 2016, Gary and I received a wonderful gift of a trip to Costa Rica. Our friends wanted us to have a great vacation, away from the stress of illness and treatment, and just have a great time. There was an event going on at the resort, and they provided all our ground expenses. All we had to do was book our flights. It was an amazing ten-day vacation that became one of our favorite places to go, and one that I will never forget. If Gary were still alive, I believe that we would be retired in Costa Rica. We loved it that much!

Being in a totally new environment, in a place where we had never been, allowed us to leave behind illness, treatment, fear, and anxiety. In this new country, we experienced many new things: a new culture, a beautiful country with a great vibe, and some amazing animals, of which our favorites were the howler monkeys. I have a video of a mama howler monkey and her baby that was so endearing to watch. I ran across this video months after Gary passed, and I was so happy that I found a video with his voice on it! It was wonderful to hear his voice again and listen to him narrating our video about these cute little creatures! One thing that's so interesting and unnerving about the howler monkeys is the sound they make! It is nothing like you would expect a monkey to sound like. It's more like a wild coyote or wolf, and when you hear the sound, it stops you in your tracks. It's amazing how such a small creature can make such a loud noise! And it was a great thing to witness, especially for two people who have struggled their whole lives with expressing their voices.

One of the greatest benefits about the resort was minimal cell and internet service! And no cable TV! We were so controlled by our electronics, me with my phone and internet and Gary with his cable TV, that we struggled for the first few days. Once we finally got past it on the fourth or fifth day, we were able to fully relax into the beauty of our surroundings. Every day we would get up and have a late morning breakfast, then head out to the secluded beach that we had to ourselves nearly the entire time. Then back to the restaurant for a late lunch, followed by an afternoon siesta!

The breakfast, lunch, and dinner menus were the same every day, and after a few days, we were tired of the limited options. Still, we didn't have to cook! I think it was partly due to our unplanned electronic detox that made us transfer that crankiness to our limited meal options!

Fortunately, we had access to a vehicle and made several trips to explore Costa Rica and find other dining options. We ziplined one day! It was a blast, and for Gary being afraid of heights, I cherished the fact that he did it with me, his daredevil wife at heart!

One day, we went with our friends to tour a cactus labyrinth. Two ladies had built this on their property, and it was an amazing creation. Most of the cactuses were seven or eight feet tall, except for a few that had to be replaced at certain times and were dwarfed by the larger ones. We laughed at how we would not want to be blindfolded or inebriated while experiencing this labyrinth! That would certainly be a prickly life lesson!

What Are The Gifts?

After so many years of traveling for business, and not having time to really experience the places I have been to, this trip reminded me how important it is to really explore, be present, and have the time to enjoy the gifts of travel and new adventures. When I decided to embark on my year of travel after Gary died, it was exactly this experience in Costa Rica that I wanted to replicate in every place that I went. A reminder to detox from electronics. Be simple. No distractions. Be present. Enjoy people. Savor nature. Remain grateful.

I also learned that I need to surround myself with great allies. A core group of extraordinary friends. Like-minded people on the same journey. People I can be myself with, who challenge me to be my highest self. Those I can have great conversations with because they value what I have to say.

Activity: Nurture Me!

- What can you do to nurture yourself? List three things and add them to your to-do list.
- Limit your time on the internet, social media, and TV. Use that time to nurture yourself.
- Ask for help! What could you use some help with? Get clear, and then find a resource.
- Say YES! Be OPEN to RECEIVE!

Gratitude, Laughter, Divine

Think about today, and answer these questions in your journal:

- What are you grateful for today?
- What made you laugh today?
- Did you feel the Divine today?

Chapter 7
Leg 5: June 2019

Gary Shares: "There's so much love in the world... It's OK for me to receive it... Reflect it... Show it... Be it."

As June arrived, I settled back in my familiar yet unfamiliar haven. Walking around my property, I found many of the garden beds needed tending. I spent time cleaning the rock walkways that Gary created, removing the crud and weeds that had collected in the grout. I used a spackling knife and wire brush to remove the buildup, kind of like getting my teeth cleaned. I was the walkway hygienist! It was just like cleaning out my yucky thoughts. I am the thinking hygienist! I had forgotten how beautiful these stone walkways were, just like I had forgotten how beautiful life can be.

I created a bouquet with the overabundance of dandelions, some ornamental grass, and branches trimmed from my Japanese maple. Beauty is everywhere. Dandelions are beautiful flowers that should be appreciated for their tenacity and abundance! Just like us, they come back even stronger. Even though we might see them as annoying weeds, their greens are great to eat, and dandelion tea is wonderful! Never judge anything, including ourselves. Everything has goodness and sweetness! Remember how fun it was to blow dandelions and make a wish!

My next adventure was in San Diego for Colette Baron-Reid's Oracle Palooza. After I checked into my room, I had dinner and a glass of wine at the hotel restaurant on Mission Bay Park: a wonderful swordfish steak over carrots, mushrooms, broccoli, and a yummy sauce beneath. The steak was topped with a green crumbed concoction that reminded me of a chia pet! And as I am never one to pass up a good dessert, I chose cheesecake with a yummy blueberry compote and another glass of wine! It was delicious!

I enjoyed the company of a heron fishing for his own dinner on the rocky shore. Another sign that Gary's with me always. I have learned to enjoy my own company and have finally gotten over the fear of what people will think of me, eating by myself. I sat outside close to the water on a rocky beach with palm trees swaying in the gentle breeze and enjoyed a lovely scene with sailboats.

After dinner, I took a long and leisurely walk around Paradise Point. Marveling at the trees with twisted trunks and branches reminded me that nature is a great example of going with the flow, working with whatever is happening around us, and creating a flexible reality in which to live our best lives. So many beautiful and vibrant flowers. I marveled at the shocking pink hibiscus, deep purple flowering trees, bright pink hydrangeas, and birds of paradise. There is so much beauty and vibrancy that we can have in our lives if we just say yes!

My cute little beach bungalow, number 274, had a big ornate scrolling wood ornament above the door. It was almost too big for the door, but it leant such a feeling of royalty, as if welcoming the queen to her abode. The workshop introduced the new Goddess card deck, and there were huge murals of many of the Goddesses hung around the room. It was wonderful to be in that divine feminine presence. I spoke to my son at one point, and he told me that he got a new husky puppy and named her Hera! What a coincidence, as Hera was one of the Goddesses in the card deck.

After the workshop, I joined my mom and daughter for a relaxing respite in Mazatlán, Mexico. This trip was another wonderful gift from a good friend, who loved Gary and always honored him as the second most handsome man in the room! He offered me his family's vacation home to heal and rest. We arrived early evening, with just enough time to take a walk along the beach and see the breathless sunset that welcomed us to Mexico, one of my favorite countries.

Our haven was a large three-bedroom suite on the top floor with a living room and kitchen, and a grand balcony with incredible views of the ocean. Every morning we experienced glorious sunrises to remind us of the promise of each day presenting itself to us. Every evening we witnessed majestic sunsets, showing us the beauty in the day that was ending with a feeling of gratitude. The moon over the sea was spectacular, especially as huge flocks of pelicans flew in formation each night, as if honoring the day and the moment. It almost seemed like we were witnessing prehistoric birds flying above us, transporting us to another space and time.

We slept in, and just before noon, we ventured out to see the city. Mexican families were enjoying their summer holiday, with many wearing matching shirts. One of the things I've always loved about the Mexican culture is their love of family. On the boardwalk, there was a huge Mazatlán sign, with each letter painted with bright colors and images. It was a favorite place for everyone to get pictures taken with the majestic ocean view in the background.

We took a bus tour through the city and sat in the top open-air section. We passed many beautiful statues and sculptures along the boardwalk: Los Peloteros, a pair of baseball players; a pair of seals; a lighthouse atop a large column with male and female gods at the bottom; jumping dolphins in a fountain; a mermaid sitting in a tower of rocks; and a woman emerging from a large shell. My favorite was a Pulmonia sculpture, honoring the fun open-air taxis that breeze around the Malecon with their Latino music pumping loudly through the speakers.

At nearby Balcones de Loma Linda, we saw a man dive from a tall rock tower with a wooden platform at the top. He would dive into the surf at just the right moment as the water was coming back in. The timing had to be exactly right. Otherwise, he would be diving into very shallow waters. I thought about how timing in life is so critical to how things turn out for us. If it's off just a smidge, it can create bigger challenges. But when it's exactly perfect, the results are wonderful! Just like the diver, you must make sure your timing is right. Then just surrender to life and take that terrifying leap! I congratulated myself for choosing me so courageously. In hindsight, I could see that my timing was perfect. Because here I was in Mexico with my two best girls living the good life! That's forward motion for sure!

We embarked on a zipline excursion with a group of ten adventurous folks. My daughter and I made it through eight ziplines high in the trees and ended with a long drop to the ground. I love anything challenging and high adrenaline. We had to jump out while they let the line loose to lower us to the ground, where a guide caught us at the bottom. I stepped right up and was the first to go! My daughter was next and was quite nervous. I got a priceless photo of her looking shocked as she was dropped! Once she got to the ground, she had the biggest smile on her face. That was my laughter find for the day!

The next stop took us to a tequila distillery. A vibrant yellow butterfly greeted us amidst the bright pink bougainvillea. In the old days, before automation, they used donkeys on a round grinder during the preparation process. It was interesting to learn that tequila is aged in barrels, just like wine. We got to taste several flavors of tequila. Mom didn't like any of them, so my daughter and I happily drank her share!

Our next excursion was a ferry ride to Sinaloa. We sailed around beautiful rock outcroppings in the ocean, with lots of caves and coves. We met a huge sea lion sunbathing on a large rock with bright green moss all around the sides. He was mostly oblivious to us. However, at the end, he lifted his huge head and greeted us!

We spent the afternoon on a busy beach where we had lunch and margaritas. My daughter and I took a boat ride on a big banana-shaped tube that had six seats. You swung your leg over and held on for dear life. It was fun being pulled out by the motorboat through the waves and out to the open sea.

We had some young adults on our boat who decided to be bold and tipped our boat upside down! That was quite a surprise and one of those moments where life smacks you right in the face, and you must decide whether to laugh, cry, or get angry. Initially, we were mad, but once we found our hats and were helped back onto the banana boat, which is hard when you have no ground to push off from, we were sucked into the laughter and enthusiasm of the kids. And glad that we were heading back to shore! We definitely needed another margarita after that!

The next day, we placed some of Gary's ashes in the ocean. Gary and I had traveled to Mexico many times, and it was bittersweet to be there without him. We each took a handful, and I reminded everyone to be mindful of the breeze before placing them in the water. We didn't want Gary being flung all over the place! We took one last walk on the beach and then made our way back to San Diego.

One place that mom really wanted to see was the Midway Museum. Initially, I didn't want to, but she's always liked naval stuff because her late brother was in the Navy. We decided to go in, and it was so much fun! We spent the whole day there. We didn't even get to finish the tour at the top of the aircraft carrier because we had spent so much time checking out all the other parts of the ship.

We did the Maxflight ride, which is a flight simulator for a fighter jet. We laughed as we were spun left and right, upside down, and in circles. When we finished, we went to the ladies' room. I've traveled all over the world and had never seen a bathroom like this. You washed your hands, and then the faucet included a hand dryer too. Super-efficient, and so military! I have a video of my mom washing and drying her hands with her hair flying all over the place and laughing like a Sports Illustrated model!

We spent a lot of time in the lower sections of the ship, learning all about how the ship was run and imagining her brother living the aircraft carrier life. It was humbling to see how our navy folks live on a ship like this. We then made it onto the deck where the fighter jets take off and land, along with a wide variety of other aircraft to see and climb into.

We spent time with a retired officer who explained how the jets landed on the aircraft carrier. Another officer shared how they took off, which was so complex yet simple. It took extreme concentration by several individuals: the pilot, those connecting the planes to the hydraulic launching system, and the officer in charge of making it all sync for a perfect takeoff. I was impressed by the procedure, just like the logistics I use in running a successful event! The fighter jets and their pilots were akin to the speakers at the many events I've produced, the stars of the show. Everyone else, plus all the procedures and platforms, are the all-important secret sauce needed to make that flight soar!

We then stopped at my favorite place in San Diego, Little Italy. Gary and I had come here many times over the years and enjoyed the ambiance and amazing cuisine. My favorites still are pistachio gelato and napoleons!

As mom headed back to Denver, I made my way to the Big Money Business Summit with Susie Carder at the Hotel Republic. I LOVED my gift bag! I've produced tons of events over the years, and this was one great goodie bag! It included a journal, water bottle, orange, snacks, mints shaped like dollar signs, a pen, and a fun sparkly clapper. I felt so loved and worthy! "Wealth is Your Birthright" was printed on the outside of the bag.

I wore the talisman necklace that I had bought on the cruise, a nautilus seashell, which was one of my and Gary's favorite shells to find. It reminds me of the infinite possibilities that life has to offer us and to always be open to receive them! The workshop was amazing and eye-opening. I met many amazing people creating their best lives. I found my business coach and mentor, Susie Carder, known as the profit coach. I knew intuitively that Susie would be an important part of my path forward. Now that I was listening to my intuition more than ever, I heard the call and said yes, please! Which meant more inspirational people added to my tribe!

I arrived home in Washington State, greeted by my son's new husky puppy, Hera. She was adorable, and I was instantly in love!

On June 25th, my mom texted me a photo with her railroad wind-chime that Gary had gotten her years earlier. Mom retired from the railroad, and Gary knew this gift would mean a lot to her. Before we went to Mexico, she told me that there had been a hummingbird dive-bombing her every time she went onto her patio. We laughed that this must be Gary making his presence known! This very wind-chime now had a hummingbird nest on it with two eggs! Several weeks later, the eggs hatched, and the hummingbirds left the nest. My mom brought the nest to me, and it's now a treasured addition to my small altar for Gary.

My next excursion was to Skamania, Washington, for a weekend workshop with Celebrate Your Life. The drive from Rainier took about three hours through some gorgeous country. One of the more memorable events was a ferry excursion on the Columbia River. The scenery was spectacular, and the tour director was amazing. If you've never been on the Columbia River, add this to your bucket list. The mountains alongside the river, the beautiful and numerous shades of green, and the wildlife are truly magnificent. We even saw a seagull's nest atop a buoy marker in the river, with two seagulls watching over it. The Bridge of the Gods, in Stevenson, Washington, is where Cheryl Strayed finished her journey from California to Washington in her wonderful memoir, *Wild*.

There were so many amazing speakers at this conference, Sunny Dawn Johnston, Denise Linn, Gregg Braden, Carolyn Myss, Dr. Sue Morter, and many more. I chose to do a zip-lining experience, and Sunny Dawn Johnston was our leader. The camaraderie and connection were profound. Supporting new friends through physically challenging obstacles was such a treat! And I found a new spiritual teacher in Sunny, who would become a valued and trusted mentor in my journey moving forward. Studying with her has opened my heart and mind to recognize all the beauty around me. More importantly, her work has shown me the beauty within myself.

On this leg of the journey, I felt I was beginning to turn the tide on the internal waves of grief that were constantly slamming my shore. I was still internalizing much of it, yet I was finding ways to release them through my evolving spiritual practice. While I had gotten back to daily meditation practice earlier in the journey, I felt like I was connecting to Spirit in a deeper way now. The daily practice of being present and aware was calming the waves and allowing me to see possibility in new ways. I no longer felt envious of the happy couples that I saw. I began to bless them for the wonderful experience they were having and blessed myself that I once had that experience too.

Flashback: November 2016-July 2017

At the end of November 2016, Gary and I were in Barcelona for a travel conference. When the conference was over, a dear friend took us to Montserrat. We walked through this exquisite monastery, viewed the Black Madonna for whom the monastery was built, and trekked up the mountain to the small chapel. My friend took a beautiful picture of Gary and me in front of that chapel, and it is one of my favorite pictures of us.

My friend had to leave early but showed us a trail along the side of the mountain that we could also explore. Gary was tired, but I convinced him we had to do it. We walked the entire path, which was adorned with sculptures and statues depicting the story of Jesus and the Stations of the Cross. It was so uplifting and inspirational, truly a feat of Divine creation. We were both filled with gratitude for having made the journey. Truly one of the most beautiful places I have seen on my travels!

In early 2017, Gary started to have trouble swallowing, and the tumor returned. He made dinner for us and we sat down to eat. Suddenly, he started sputtering, and he sprang up and ran to the bathroom and coughed everything up. It had gotten caught in his throat, unable to go down, not only because of the tumor pushing into his esophagus, but also because he had no saliva to help move it through. And that's when he told me what was going on, that he had choked on his food several times while I was gone. I was so worried that he was going to have an emergency while I was away, and there would be nobody there with him. We decided that any time I was traveling, a family member would come and stay with him.

He also shared that the last time he joined me on a trip, while he was waiting for his flight, he decided to eat at an airport restaurant. He sat at the bar next to another gentleman, and they got to talking. When his food arrived, he tried to eat and immediately threw it all up into his napkin. He was so embarrassed and apologized profusely to his companion. My heart ached for him.

We decided that it would be best for Gary not to eat unless I was home. We had breakfast together in the morning, then I went to the office, which was only a mile away. I would then come home for a short lunch, go back to work, and then come back home for dinner. Then I would finish whatever work I had for the day, either from home or back at the office. It was very tiring for me, yet it wasn't worth the risk for him to eat on his own. Even though I worked so close to home, it wasn't enough time to get home if he was suffocating on his food.

Around mid-July, we took a trip to Tucson to see my son. It was a difficult trip for Gary. He spent most of his time in the hotel room because he just didn't have the energy to do anything. The few times that he felt up to join us for a meal, he couldn't eat anything. His weight was dropping rapidly, and I could see his energy diminishing daily. At one point, he was in so much pain and was trying to take some medication, and he couldn't even swallow a small pill.

One day, my son and I toured an underground cave in Tucson. Previously, he had shared with me some interesting dreams and meditations he had in the previous weeks. We talked about those again while driving to the cave. A memorable experience in the cave confirmed that Spirit was preparing us for some major transitions ahead.

We knew that Gary was gravely ill, but we were hopeful for a miracle healing. Little did we know that in less than a year, he would be gone. Additionally, within days after we got back from Tucson, we tragically lost an amazing friend from a senseless murder. Gary was distraught about this. He lamented that he should have been taken instead, given his condition. It was the first time that he had spoken out loud about his mortality.

What Are The Gifts?

This trip really taught me about feeling the Divine in every place that we went. Having gone to Montserrat and experiencing the energy of that holy place was the highlight of this trip for us. Every trip after that, I strove to see and feel the Divine in all my travels. That's not to say I hadn't found any before, because I have seen many amazing churches, cathedrals, and sacred places. What was different in Montserrat was that I had the time to really explore and be present. I wasn't rushed to get through it because of limited time due to work commitments. It's amazing what having the freedom to explore and not rushing can do for you to experience seeing and feeling the Divine!

Our lives can change so rapidly, sometimes in the blink of an eye. Most times, we are not prepared for the change and its aftermath. When we have a challenging situation in our lives, we scramble trying to deal with it while also trying to maintain the status quo with our jobs, our relationships, and our communities. Usually, we don't have a good way of balancing our needs against these challenges. I had to learn how to rearrange my work commitments to support Gary's health crisis. And how to deal with the plethora of emotions that came along with that sacrifice: anger, guilt, sadness, fear of missing out, and fear of the worst-case scenario—death.

Learning how to rearrange and reframe during Gary's illness afforded me the experience to take it to the next step after his death, which was leaving my job. During my year of travel, traveling basically replaced my job. I was able to balance the travel more easily with my personal inner work and find a way to marry the two in a harmonious way. When I was ready to jump back into work, I was more easily able to envision what I wanted for my new career in a way that complemented my inner journey.

When we learn how to float between our personal and professional lives more effortlessly and harmoniously, we can navigate challenges more successfully.

Activity: New Accomplishments

Think of someone important to you that died. Or an experience that is causing you pain.

- What three things did you love about them or the situation?
- What three good things have you done, learned, or accomplished since their death or the experience? It can be simple, examples; traveled by yourself, re-established a favorite hobby, mowed the lawn, house repairs, met new friends, volunteering, financial, etc.

Gratitude, Laughter, Divine

Think about today, and answer these questions in your journal:

- What are you grateful for today?
- What made you laugh today?
- Did you feel the Divine today?

Chapter 8
Leg 6: July-August 2019

Gary Shares: "We contribute to the world in unforeseen ways that bring joy, peace, and new adventure."

As I was driving home from Skamania, I pulled over in Washougal for one last picturesque goodbye to the Columbia River at Cape Horn. It was truly breathtaking. I'm always amazed at the many shades of green that are present in the Pacific Northwest, from exceptionally light to nearly neon, accented with the deepest of greens. All nurtured and loved by the overcast and cloudy skies, the rainy mists, and the occasional presence of the sun! As July begins, the sun will be more present through the summer and usually through September, before the rains arrive to take back their domain for the many months to come.

As I took in the beauty, I contemplated how far I had come since Gary's death. I had been on the road for four months, and every day was a step further away from Gary. As I savored in the many shades of green, I realized that grief also has many shades. Each day could be so different.

The bright neon green is like the rawness of grief when it first arrives. That rawness returned in full force when I arrived back at our home of nearly twenty-one years. Where we lived, loved, and shared the end of his life together. I was now alone. One day, I did a meditation attempting to replace the last horrific memories of his cancer-ridden body with images of him at his most vibrant. Suddenly, I was taken into his emaciated body and felt the pain and choking of the tumor. I felt the panic of being unable to breathe. I felt the feelings that he felt as he came to terms that his life was almost over. The knowledge that his time was short, and no amount of begging God was going to change the outcome. I realized on a deep physical level how horrible his cancer was. I also realized on a deep emotional level how much despair he was feeling in the days leading up to his decision that it was time to surrender. I realized that once he made the decision to surrender, a calming peace came over him.

I was not able to see any of these things as they happened in real time. Our minds have a way of distracting us from the raw truths of mortality in real time. Looking back on it now, I believe that was the only way I could muster the courage to be strong for him and serve him to the best of my ability. I could not have cared for him through all the horribleness if I allowed myself to truly feel my sadness and anger in those moments. My survival mechanism kicked in and pushed those feelings deep into my body. My body, being the ever-faithful servant, held those energies courageously and quietly. My body shielded me from the pain as best it could, but it couldn't hold it forever. The explosion was appendicitis. My body sacrificed part of itself for me. It was now obvious that those emotions were still in my body. I had not refilled the empty space that my appendix left with a higher vibrational energy of healing. That space was still attracting the lower vibrational energy because that's what it knew. Now it was time to really feel those feelings. The anger and rage passed through me as I relived

Gary's physical and emotional trauma. His trauma became my trauma, and just as he surrendered that last week, it was now my turn to surrender that energy to God.

I allowed God to fill me up with understanding and compassion. I also allowed myself benevolence and mercy for not being able to hear my body's cries for help. This was a capstone moment for me. I was ready to start listening to my body every day. As pain or discomfort arose, I was getting better at bringing my awareness to my body much quicker. There were still many times I was oblivious, especially as life got stressful. Yet my body was now aware that I was listening better, and it doesn't give up as easily.

Just like nurturing our relationships with our family and friends, we must nurture our relationship with our bodies. When we do that, we rebuild the trust and our health blooms. We move into the warm, soft shades of green that allow us to navigate our landscape calmly and confidently. We flow more easily through life, like the breeze that rustles through the aspen leaves and allows their voices to be heard.

We mature more gracefully into our higher essence as we enter these deeper shades of green. These richer shades embody compassion and transform knowledge into wisdom. It becomes easier to sail through the waves of grief that come. Amazingly, the waves become smaller because our presence has grown larger. We have rooted deeply into the earth while at the same time reaching higher toward the sun. The depths of our roots and the height of our branches are balanced by our heart. And when our heart is balanced, we bring joy back in.

I'm glad to be home for the summer, and I'm intent on making the best of it. I quickly realized that I'm not fearful or worried that Gary died in this house. I want to be here, where we created many years of memories, not to mention Gary's beautiful handiwork in the yard and garden.

In early July, mom sent me a photo of the newly hatched hummingbirds in the wind chime nest! So adorable to see their delicate long beaks poking out of the nest, waiting for momma to feed them. My hummingbird friend with the red throat often returned to say hi!

I enjoyed spending time with my son's three huskies, Zeus, Xena, and Hera, the newest addition, and the most adorable puppy. She's lighter colored, with whites and grays and a bit of tan in her face. Her best feature is her big creamy white ears outlined in a deep gray. Her face is framed with the cutest outline above her mesmerizing amber eyes. It almost looks like a person with its arms over her eyes, dark gray accents where the elbows would be, and broad shoulders with a head outlined in gray like a halo. It looks like she is being hugged by an angel! Maybe it's her namesake, the Goddess Hera, the wife of Zeus. My son's plan was to breed her with Zeus; thus, the name Hera came to be.

One Saturday, I sat on the porch with my coffee and enjoyed the birds playing in Gary's favorite tree. There are so many of them, chirping away, excited for the new day, even though it's drizzly. This tree is a red Japanese maple that graces the front yard. It stands as a welcome to the stone steps leading down to the fire pit, surrounded by stone beds with many trees, including my favorite Weeping Sequoia.

There are wide stone steps leading up on the other side that have succulents growing along the backs of the steps. You can sit on the stone bench on the north side of the fire pit, which is flanked by another Japanese maple and a wispy, feathery evergreen that looks so soft, but is scratchy to the touch. It reminds me of a beautiful woman who looks soft and flowy, but silently has her defenses ready.

I spent some time going through Gary's photos. I found one of him and his brother in San Diego, both working for the post office as mail carriers. They are smiling big, with their 80's hair, donning their uniforms of light blue short-sleeved button-up shirts and darker blue shorts, finished with long dark socks! Gary has his sunglasses hanging around his neck with his mailbag on his right shoulder. This would have been before Gary's accident. I sure wish he had delivered my mail! It was fun to send this photo to his brother!

I enjoyed watching my son ride his quad around the property, laughing as he did wheelies and side wheelies and gleefully played like a child again. At one point during a wheelie, the quad tipped too far back and stopped with its front wheels straight up in the air. He looked up at me in the window and sheepishly smiled, wondering if mom saw him!

A ladybug visited and was a harbinger for the arrival of my author's copy of *Inspirations*! My first published chapter! I wrote about my experience after Gary's death. My story is on page 175, *A Reluctant Widow's Grateful Journey*. As I was recording a book launch video with my newly arrived book, a hummingbird flew right in front of me! A good sign!

The big test was upon me, as I spent more than two months at home. I was quite road-weary and excited to be home with nothing to do and nowhere to be. I began to consider recreating my space to bring in fresh energy. I had tried before but always felt guilty about changing anything, like I was somehow dishonoring Gary.

This time I felt empowered to make small changes to make it more mine. After years of deferring to him, now I had all the power! And it was fun! For our bedroom, I bought a fun gray comforter with flouncy edges, adding simple floral pillows. I found a plush rug with a sea turtle swimming through the ocean over several shades of coral. Gary loved sea turtles. To me, the rug symbolizes Gary's freedom. It makes me smile every time I look at it. Then I completely took over the closets and drawers! It felt good to freshen it up, like I was letting go of what was, to create room for what's to come!

I unwrapped new furniture that had been stored in the garage for months because I felt guilty replacing Gary's much-loved sectional. I had planned to donate the sectional to my work, but I just kept thinking that Gary would be all alone on his couch at the office! Funny how our minds work. Months earlier, my mom had lovingly packed all of Gary's clothes for me, sorting them by size and style in clear plastic bins. These were still in the garage over a year after his death. It took me that long to be ready to do anything with them. I saved several of his beloved plaid shirts to someday make a quilt. One sunny summer day, my son and I took all the clothes to a church that distributed clothing to people in need.

I rearranged my office, grateful for the big desk that Gary had refurbished for me with his talented tile work. My son and I repainted the guest bedroom and added new furniture and bedding in anticipation of the arrival of our Dutch friends.

In early August, my friends from Holland arrived. We drove to Vancouver, Canada, to visit a beautiful family whom I've known for years through our spiritual circles. It was celebration week for LGBTQ, so the energy was vibrant and fun and highly creative and colorful! We stayed at a sweet and wonderfully comfortable hotel located in the heart of the city. Vancouver is a beautiful, cosmopolitan city, right on the water, with so many walking trails and paths. We had dinner on Granville Island. What a beautiful evening, filled with food, wine, and most importantly, connection with good friends!

We spent the next day in the West End and visited the Happy Man statues. We had such fun mimicking the statues and taking hilarious pictures. On a short concrete semi-circular wall around the statues, it states: *May this sculpture inspire laughter, playfulness, and joy in all who experience it.* It certainly inspired laughter, playfulness, and joy for us as we experienced it together! I submitted one of the photos for the contest the hotel was running, and I won a two-night stay! We ended our visit with lunch and beers at an outside cafe. How wonderful to celebrate life with great friends in great cities!

On the drive back to the states, my friends dropped me off at a hotel in Belleview, Washington. I was to be on the Gratitude Cafe radio show the next day to promote the

Inspirations book launch with one of my co-authors. I had never met her and was a little nervous sharing a hotel room with someone I'd only met online. We became fast friends, and she's now one of my dearest friends. Connections happen everywhere. You just need to have an open heart!

We met up with another friend at a coffee shop in Pike Place Market. From the menu, I ordered Garry's Oatmeal, which was made from thick-cut oats served with golden raisins, dark brown sugar, and milk on the side with fresh fruit. What a sweet coincidence, as Gary made the best oatmeal using real oats and blueberries, raspberries, and blackberries, with walnuts, raisins, milk, and honey or brown sugar mixed in! This was accompanied, of course, by a yummy cappuccino with a heart in the foam!

My friend and I strolled through the market and took pictures of our book with the pig sculpture near the fish market. We found a beautiful hummingbird poster and another one with hummingbirds of Costa Rica, which was one of my best vacations with Gary. We leisurely strolled towards the train station, as I was taking the Amtrak back home later that day. We found a little bar with outdoor seating to enjoy a beer and toasted to our new adventures as authors and friends. We launched a video with our 101 Days of Inspiration Challenge, encouraging people to post pictures of things that inspire them.

I splurged and bought myself a business class ticket! I really enjoyed the train ride. It was a nice time to reflect on my new track in life and to enjoy the scenery passing by. The nearly two-hour ride left from Seattle at King Street Station went through Kent, The Narrows in Tacoma, Steilacoom, and finally, my destination at the Olympia-Lacey station.

Two days after the book launch, I officially became an International Amazon Bestselling author! I never thought of myself as a writer, but when the opportunity presented itself to write a chapter in a collaborative book, I decided to act! It also enfolded me into a wonderful group of writers led by my incredible publisher, As You Wish Publishing.

One day, I got to witness my cat Gizmo bringing a live mouse to the door. I tensely watched as he ate nearly everything, leaving just a small organ on the doormat. Usually, we see some internal organs and fur, maybe a tail and a foot. Maybe he was putting on a show for me since he was allowing me to watch, or maybe it was just a super tasty mouse. Gizmo has always been a great hunter and keeps our property free from rodents. Up until Gary died, he had always been an outdoor cat, as Gary was allergic. I decided it would be nice to have a companion inside, and I bought him a bed and brought him in at night. During the day, he would be outside to nap in the barn or greenhouse and hunt. He's 15 and a little thinner now. Of all our cats we've had over the years, he's been around the longest and is our favorite of the bunch! His preferred place to rest is either at the foot of Gary's chair or underneath it. This was the zero-gravity chair where Gary spent the last several months of his life, as due to the trach, he could no longer sleep in the bed. I'm positive Gizmo feels Gary here, as he's got that "Giz wizdom!"

August 19th marked Gary's second birthday without him. He would have been 64. I so wish he could sing that

Beatles song to me: *When I'm 64*. I played it for him several times today! As if to celebrate him, two hummingbirds met at the feeder, sharing it peacefully, one on either side. Writing August 19 was a stark reminder of his illness. For every medical appointment, we checked in by his birthdate. We were always saying 8/19/55. I guess being recognized by your birthdate is better than a random number. At least it's affirming the amazing moment Gary was born!

Here's a crazy sign of Gary's continued presence in my life. Yesterday there was a Coca-Cola bottle cap on my sofa! We don't drink Coke, and no one had been in the house other than my son and me. When Gary and I would go to Mexico, our favorite drink besides El Modelo beer or margaritas was Coke in bottles! Coke tastes so much better in Mexico!

This memory popped up on my Facebook feed today from 2009, a quote from Desiderius Erasmus: "If you keep thinking about what you want to do or what you hope will happen, you don't do it, and it doesn't happen."

It's so true, isn't it? Action is the one key ingredient to moving through and beyond grief. All the thinking in the world, even if it's good, will not change anything if you choose to stay in place.

Flashback: July-August 2017

Gary and I decided to go to Brazil for two weeks in late July 2017. I had a few trips prior to that, and on one of my trips to Cancun, a good friend, who was a coach and healer, had wanted Gary to come to Minnesota to do some healing work with her. She believed that since he was born in

Minnesota, being where he was born could help facilitate his healing. She also thought that going to Brazil was an amazing idea, which set the tone for us to decide to go, as we trusted her guidance.

I scrambled to get our Brazilian visas and passports ready to go. I was concerned if it was even safe for Gary to travel during this time. I connected with our Brazilian guide that we hired to support us, and I voiced my concern. She shared with me that she felt intuitively that he would be fine, and to just get there as quickly as we could.

We finally got all our travel paperwork completed and boarded our flights to Brazil. The swelling in his neck, jaw, and chin increased while we were there, and the tumor was slowly increasing in size. It was very disconcerting, and at one point, he woke up in the evening and was very dizzy and disoriented. I honestly thought this was the end. He also thought it was the end, but he pulled through, and things started to get better. The tumor started to grow from a small marble size to a shooter marble size. After we had been there a week and had some healing sessions, it started to drain, which we thought was a good sign. However, the pain was increasing, and it was getting harder for him to swallow food. One day, after the healing service, we went and had soup in the community kitchen. Gary tried to eat and immediately threw up in front of everyone. I think I was more embarrassed than he was. Then I was so proud of him for even attempting to eat in front of all these people. After all, everyone there needed some form of healing. They were all so loving and compassionate with him, as he was one of their brothers in need of love and support.

We began our treatment with crystal light therapy. I laid on a massage table on my back while a light fixture with seven colored crystal lights pointed at each of my seven chakra centers, intermittently blinking on and off. I meditated while beautiful music played softly. After our first session, I walked Gary back to the room so he could rest. I went back and sat in the garden for meditation. It was a profound experience where I heard these instructions:

To maintain healthy outer vision, you must maintain healthy inner vision. That means looking at every situation from every perspective before making any decisions. Decisions or choices always must be made with the highest good of all. You must look without judgment, without fear, without anger, without malice, without guilt. Even if someone has wronged you, you must look at it from their perspective. Why did they do that to you? Find a way to forgiveness, understand if they are acting out against you. Be clear that there could be a valid reason, and if there is, reflect within yourself on how you could avoid someone doing that again. If you honestly believe there is no reason, then realize they're calling out for love, and that's the only way they know how. Maybe the very thing they need is for you to love them regardless. That doesn't mean you condone it; you just have compassion. That's a true master's way. There is always room to love. Be very vigilant in your perspectives. Life is about demonstrating grace. All I want to be is grace. All are worthy of healing.

I had many weird dreams over the next few days about various challenging people and situations. One morning when I woke up, I was reminded that as we love and honor

God, we love and honor ourselves. And that everyone has value, everyone is part of God, and NO ONE is left out.

After another crystal light session, I gleaned this message: *When you are having challenges with people, you need to be clear with them for their sake. For yourself, being clear with them helps to set boundaries. Ignoring an issue or person is a judgment. It is a judgment that dishonors everyone, but mostly affects the one who is doing the ignoring. Just like forgiveness, it most affects the one who forgives.*

During the second week, we each did another crystal light session. Our friend who had died the previous month came to Gary and hugged him from behind. He could smell her hair. He was so comforted to know that she was still there, helping with his healing from beyond.

What Are The Gifts?

One of the great things that I learned while we were in Brazil was the art of disconnecting and going within. I also went in search of healing for my eyes, and part of my protocol was an eight-day fast from my phone and laptop. Initially, it was difficult because I had a very demanding job, and I was so used to being super busy all the time. Those two weeks in Brazil provided me the ability to see what it's like to disconnect from work, the internet, and social media. To remember what life is like without constant emails and phone calls. To start enjoying the peace and the silence, and most importantly, remembering how to connect with my inner self. We spent many days in meditation for three and four hours at a time, mostly on my own because Gary was not able to sit for that long. We had several sessions of crystal light healing, which were magical. And I had an incredible experience with people I did not know at a sacred waterfall. I experienced many amazing insights, visions, and dreams, all of which prepared me for the challenging times to come.

This experience of disconnecting for eight days helped me with the transition of disconnecting from all that had consumed me for the last several years. It allowed me to know how to be present and enjoy my travels while also getting to know myself. It supported me when I felt it was time to change up my home and create an environment to support the new me that was emerging.

Activity: Space Revamp

- Rework your physical environment. Change it up.
- Check out Feng Shui, declutter, rearrange furniture, add plants, etc.
- Create a sacred space for yourself.
- Journal how you felt before and after.

Gratitude, Laughter, Divine

Think about today, and answer these questions in your journal:

- What are you grateful for today?
- What made you laugh today?
- Did you feel the Divine today?

Chapter 9
Leg 7: Early September 2019

Gary Shares: "To live with one's own truth is to be at home with oneself."

September 3rd saw mom and me jetting off to Europe, where we were joined by my daughter. We spent a week in Amsterdam at a friend's flat in the city. I had been to Amsterdam several times before, yet never long enough to really experience the city. We had a great time going to museums, walking along the canals, and seeing the windmills while basking in the love of my beloved Dutch friends. We even got them out to places they had never been to in their own city!

If you can't or don't like to travel, do mini excursions in your own city! I have made a pact with myself that when I'm home, I will check out new things in my own backyard. You don't have to travel far and wide, as beauty and divinity exist everywhere and in every moment.

We walked around the Leidsegracht neighborhood when we first arrived. As we strolled past the many beautiful houses along the canal, I noticed a tall, stately gray house with six stories. All the many windows were painted in white trim, which made for an exceptionally clean and contemporary building. The most intriguing thing for me was that just above the second-floor middle window was the word "Archangel" in white! I had been working a lot with the

Archangels in the last few months, so this was a nice sign to welcome us to Amsterdam!

In the Canal Belt, I snapped an interesting picture of a wall with typical Dutch artwork in blue and white, with the city line in the clouds and a windmill to the right. In between was a ballerina, and next to her were the words "Think Different." This was a confirmation for me of what I was endeavoring to do daily to move through my grief: **do something different every day.**

In Prinsengracht, we saw two houses that were leaning away from each other and had been rejoined together with some sort of black material to stabilize them. You see this all over the city since Amsterdam is below sea level.

We finally got to our flat, which was a cute one-bedroom on the fifth floor, and no elevator! We were so grateful for this wonderful place to stay right in the center of the city, close to all the action and within walking distance of all the amazing canals.

We slept in the next morning due to jet lag, then ventured out for a walk to find food. We came upon a cute restaurant where we had Dutch pancakes. Mine was a chocolate banana pancake with ice cream called Bananasplit Pannenkoek. It was way too much food, but I ate it all! Mom had the more traditional apple and ham pancake, called Pannenkoek Appel En Spek.

We walked by the Anne Frank House and continued our stroll through the Canal Belt and Jordaan. We happened upon the Tulip Museum, where we were greeted by a myriad of tulip varieties. We learned the tulip had its origins in the Tian Shan Mountains, or the heavenly mountains, in Central

Asia. The display said, *Here on the roof of the Earth, the tulip came to symbolize birth, life, and fertility in the minds of those who shared its home.* The tulip was considered the holiest of flowers. It literally meant the flower of God in Arabic script, as Laleh. The Turkish word for tulip is written in the same letters as Allah; tulip is oJlJ, while Allah is oJJl. The name tulip is the Latinized version of the Turkish word for turban because the flower's shape was thought to resemble a turban.

Next, we hopped on a canal cruise and sailed past spectacular buildings. People were happily sitting on the canal walls dangling their feet, while many more rode by on their bicycles. There were many houseboats and boats, one that was called, *Living Life.* Exactly what we were doing!

We passed the flower market where there was a humorous painting of Vincent Van Gogh. It said, "Vincent was here 1877," and he was sporting just one ear! After the cruise was done, we strolled through the flower market to see many beautiful flowers, so much more than just tulips.

One day, we toured the Royal Palace of Amsterdam. Outside in Dam Square, there were amazing bubble artists thrilling adults and children alike with their huge bubble wands that created a mass of bubbles. It was drizzling, so we decided to take a horse and buggy tour, much to the chagrin of our Dutch friends. I believe one of them said, "You'll never catch me dead in one of those," when I enthusiastically texted a picture! We began the ride in Dam Square, through Herengracht and back to the square. It was a lovely and restful way to see the city!

Great Loss, Greater Love

I had been journaling every day since I started traveling, which was helping me to be mindful and present. I happened to skip one day while in Amsterdam, and my body pains and fears came right back. It was so immediate, like they were just waiting for a crack in the armor to jump in. A great dinner with our friends reminded me how blessed I am and how loved. I'm proud of myself today! For being aware of the real me. For listening to my body. And for remembering how powerful I am. It takes the same amount of energy to feel bad as it does to feel good!

Our friends joined us for a leisurely walk along the canals. We enjoyed watching a dragon boat race. Each boat had a drummer at the head facing the crew, with the leader standing at the rear. It was fun to watch them paddle their oars to the steady beat of the drummers.

Later we hopped in the car and drove to the windmills in Zaandam, Zaanse Schans. The size of the windmills was incredible! The blades were massive. Some of the windmills were used to grind rocks and sand, some for wheat and grains. The intricacy involved in these grinding machines was mind-boggling. We finished the day, sharing a delicious Iranian dinner at another friend's house near The Hague.

A few days later, my daughter arrived. We went to the Anne Frank Museum, where my Dutch friends had not been, by the way! Remember my point about exploring our own backyard? The entire tour was so somber and heavy. How the Frank family survived twenty-five months in hiding has always been unbelievable. Being in quarantine during the 2020 pandemic has given us just a tiny glimpse into what they experienced.

Five days after our arrival in Amsterdam, it was time to say goodbye to our beloved friends, and what better way than a traditional Dutch lunch! Then we were off to Barcelona, one of my favorite cities. We landed amid heavy rains and thunderstorms, and upon arrival at my good friend's apartment, we found it flooded. Our first several hours were spent getting the place cleaned up. Regardless, it was a great tradeoff for a wonderful place to stay near the beach, in La Vila Olímpica. I also got to see her beautiful momma again because of the flooding! Bonus!

The next day, we did one of my favorite things and hopped on a tour bus with friends! Through the rainy bus ride, we saw all the beauty that is Barcelona. I had been here several times on business, so it was great to have the time to explore. Later, we shared dinner with more friends.

We spent a day walking around Catalonia Square. It was still rainy and cool, so we hopped on another tour bus, and finally, blue skies and sun! We rode through the Passeig de Gràcia, one of the city's most important shopping and business districts. We passed the Sagrada Familia, Antoni Gaudi's awe-inspiring church, still under construction since 1882, with plans to be completed in 2026. Next, we saw Tibidabo, where the Sagrat Cor church sits atop the hill. This church only took sixty years to complete!

With the tour done, we went to my favorite place in Barcelona, La Rambla. It's nearly a mile-long, tree-lined street with wonderful shops and restaurants. There's even more to discover within the many side streets. It was a holiday, and many people were wearing Catalonian flags. We completed our stroll with a walk down to the docks and beach. A guy and his dog entertained us playing frisbee, executing flips and long graceful runs. It was beautiful on the beach, with the famous W Hotel and its interesting half-moon shape as a backdrop. Our Barceloneta Beach stroll ended with a cool sandcastle, complete with burning candles in the two doorways.

After three days in Barcelona, we traveled to Bordeaux, France, for a friend's wedding. We arrived in beautiful weather and stayed in a wonderful little flat in the city on the Rue Georges Bonnac. There were cobblestone streets everywhere around us, with wonderful shops and cafes. And even a Starbucks across the street from our flat!

We walked to the Garrone River, where we found the beautiful Vieille Ville Fountain. We enjoyed a water feature across the street that mists as you walk across it, so refreshing on this hot day. There was an abundance of beautiful architecture, churches, and flowers like morning glories.

We stopped in an eclectic art shop that was full of bulldogs. There were many sizes of the same shape, in many colorful versions. We also saw many interesting kinds of furniture, including a big wooden Buddha statue. We strolled along the Port Autonome de Bordeaux, with its bridge over the river that raises for ships to pass through. We took a wine cruise on the river, where we enjoyed yummy wine and cheese amidst a beautiful sunset. After the cruise, we walked through the biggest wine collection I've ever seen, with two stories of wine on every wall!

The next day found us sightseeing again. We saw the Cathedrale Saint-Andre church, with its beautiful spires. At the Saint-Michel church, we lit long candles for Gary, Brad, and Uncle Lenny. My daughter and I climbed up the old tower, with gargoyles everywhere! We laughed as we were reminded of one of the kids' favorite Disney movies, The Hunchback of Notre Dame. The view from the top was amazing, with a 360-degree view of the entire city. As the sun went down, we went back to the fountain, which was lit up beautifully. We crossed the street to the misting fountain and walked in the mist and darkness, with the colorful streetlamps illuminating our walk. The streets were full of happy people enjoying the evening.

Two days later, my mom and daughter took the train to Paris. My Dutch friends had joined me in Bordeaux for the wedding. We drove about an hour through the beautiful French countryside, passing many vineyards along the way. The wedding was in Soussans, a beautiful winery and vineyard. Everyone was dressed in white for the festivities. The wedding chairs were set in a circular pattern that led to an open area in the center where the groom waited for the bride. They met each other in the center and did a little dance around each other, ending in a hug. They honored the elements at each point of the compass and brought their beautiful baby girl into the center with them. It was a beautiful ceremony honoring the earth, Spirit, love, and family. We each had a wand with a bell and ribbon that we shook in celebration. Toasting the couple outside was then followed by dinner and dancing. It was such a beautiful and fun night. I thought it might be hard going to a wedding as a widow. But the love and joy were so refreshing to see, a reminder that love is everywhere, in all things, in all times, forever in our grasp.

The day following the wedding, I took the train to Paris to meet up with my girls. They had a great time together in this beautiful city. I met them at the airport, and we all left France: my daughter flew back to the states, while mom and I finished our European vacation in London.

We walked in Kensington Gardens, which was just across the street from our hotel. The Queen Victoria statue was beautiful, surrounded by a pond filled with water lilies and ornamental grasses. "200 Years" was spelled out with maroon-colored succulents in the white rocks, as 2019 marked two-hundred years since her birth. The gate leading to the palace was very ornate and grand, gilded in gold. There were swans everywhere.

We toured Kensington Palace, and the King's grand staircase was truly grand. This is where Queen Victoria grew up. She was a tiny queen, standing just five feet tall. When her beloved Prince Albert died when she was forty-two, she wore black for the rest of her life. We visited the monument she had built for Albert, which was truly spectacular. It was in a bit of disrepair, and we couldn't get close to it due to the fence surrounding it. It was near Albert Hall, which you might remember Paul McCartney singing in *A Day in the Life*, "Now you know how many holes it takes to fill the Albert Hall." Yes, it turned me on!

Our next adventure found us in the stables at Buckingham Palace, where we met some of the Queen's horses. One of them is named Svejk, born in Hungary in 2009, and was featured in the 2015 film Ben Hur. We saw all the carriages, some quite simple but most very ornate. We even got to sit in one! The gold carriage that the Queen rode in for her coronation was over the top ornate and super heavy! Then we were on our way to tour the inside of the palace. We walked through the throne room, the grand staircase, numerous reception rooms and saw many royal portraits and other works of art. In between the tours, we enjoyed tea and crumpets with clotted cream in a sweet café next to the palace.

After the tours, we hung out at the gate for a while to watch the guards. There were many unicorn statues, and I wondered what all the ER II symbols around the gates meant. I knew part of it was Elizabeth II. But what was R for? Googling it, I found it stands for Elizabeth Regina II, Regina being the Latin word for Queen.

One day, we walked around Hyde Park. The last time I was in Hyde Park was November 2016, where I bought the journal for Gary that I mentioned in the introduction. It was a nice full-circle moment to be back nearly three years later with his journal.

With our London adventure complete, we flew back to Amsterdam for one final day with our Dutchies! Then we made the long flight back to Washington State.

What a great two weeks, celebrating friends, seeing new things, feeling new emotions, and being celebrated and honored by friends who helped love me through this grieving process. I was grateful to spend time with my mom and daughter to provide them the opportunity to see more of this beautiful world.

An entry in my journal toward the end of September says: *I haven't written in here for ten days! I have been aware of Spirit in my thoughts every day and did my best to stay present. When I find myself worrying or fretting about things I can't control, I was quickly aware of it and changed my perspective. I'm getting so much better at that! I noticed that there's not as much emotional charge as before! Good for me!*

Reading those words, I think to myself: I am proud of me! I am powerful and in control!

Flashback: August-September 2017

On August 29, 2017, I arrived home from work to find Gary nervously waiting for me. I could tell that he was more agitated than usual. He had a resignation about him that was a little disconcerting. He told me that he was now just 135 pounds and worried about not being able to keep weight on. He now could not get any food down his throat. He had finally made the decision to go to the hospital and get a feeding tube. He was sure it would be a temporary thing while he continued his healing work on the cancer. I had suggested many times over the last few months that he should see a doctor, but he always adamantly said no. Each time I suggested it, I knew he felt I was losing hope in his efforts to heal. While grateful that he was willing to seek medical attention, I knew that his making this decision meant things were awfully bad.

We packed a small bag for him and headed for the hospital. As we entered the ER, a sense of foreboding gripped me. It was a heroic effort to remain calm and stay strong for him. We were immediately sent to an intake room, I'm sure, because of his appearance. Each time we spoke to a staff member, I could feel the unspoken question: Why did you wait so long to bring him to us? The shame and guilt rushed over me. I had always honored Gary's desire to avoid mainstream medicine at all costs. And now the cost was his life.

We had assumed that a feeding tube would be a simple procedure but soon learned the grim news after he returned from the MRI. The tumor, which originated in the back of his tongue, had now spread to his jaw and neck. Not only had it closed the esophagus, but it was also pushing against the trachea leaving only a tiny opening for air to get through. Because of his compromised airway, they could not insert a feeding tube without first doing a tracheostomy. Confident that both procedures would be temporary, Gary signed the papers to proceed.

They moved us to a nice private room on the third floor. Then the prepping process began. We changed him into the hospital gown and got him into the hospital bed. A team of nurses came in to take his vitals, insert an IV, and stock the room with all the supplies we would need after the surgeries. Once he was ready, then began the agonizing wait for the team that would escort him to the operating room.

Many years ago, my grandfather had a laryngectomy. A stoma was put in his neck to enable breathing. He lost his vocal cords and had to use a microphone-like device held near his throat to emit sound. Fearing this might happen to my husband, I recorded him speaking before they wheeled him off to surgery. As it turned out, Gary's situation was a bit different, and his vocal cords remained intact. Unlike my grandfather's laryngectomy stoma, Gary's would require a trach tube to always be inserted in his stoma. There was a removable valve that could be attached to the trach tube, which allowed air to flow through his vocal cords, enabling him to speak with his own voice. What a relief! I had never seen Gary more excited to speak out loud!

Next, they inserted the feeding tube into his abdomen. Now we had to deal with two tubes and work on regulating his nutritional needs.

A couple days later, an oncologist came to see us about further treatment. He recommended chemotherapy and radiation. Gary was adamant that he wanted no more radiation, but he reluctantly agreed to chemotherapy with the promise that after two weeks, he could switch to immune-therapy. At the time, immunotherapy was not approved unless two courses of chemotherapy were completed.

We spent two weeks in the hospital, where I slept on a small bed next to Gary. The staff brought me an extra table to set up a work area for me. Yes, I kept working. It was a needed distraction from all the seriousness surrounding us. We received so many well-wishes during our stay. The hospital staff was amazing, especially considering that this floor was the cancer floor. Gary was so well-cared for during this difficult time, while his body adjusted to all the devastating changes inflicted on it in the span of two weeks.

When the chemo started, I wrote positive words on the chemo bag. When his immune system was at its most compromised, our room became labeled as a warning zone upon entry. No one was allowed in without a mask. Interesting that in about two and a half years' time, we would be wearing them in our daily lives as the 2020 pandemic roared in.

What Are The Gifts?

Life can be short or long, yet it always has an ending. As my spiritual teacher says, there are only two sure things when we come into this life; the day we are born, and the day we die. All the details, including how we die, are all unknown. It's up to us to fill in the details about how our lives will progress. Whether we know it or not, we make choices that affect how our lives will unfold and even how we will die.

Gary knew that his emotional challenges led to his illness. All his life, he struggled with expressing himself. Holding that volatile energy in his throat area ultimately led to the cancer that ended his life. His choice not to express himself led to how his death expressed itself. Through his life and death, I have learned about the importance and power of my voice, expressed or not. I have chosen to give myself the gift of expression. This book is one of those gifts for me. It's also a gift for Gary since he was not able to share his story.

We all have a story to share, and it's our responsibility to share it. Our way of expression is unique to us. There will be people for whom our stories will open doors to guide them in the direction of their healing and expression. It's a ripple effect that supports all of us in experiencing our highest version of life.

Activity: Flip Your Beliefs

- List three beliefs that are not supporting you. Example: I'm not creative.

- Rewrite them in a positive way. Example: Creativity comes easily to me.
- Add the new re-written versions to your daily meditation/prayer practice. Post them on sticky notes on your mirror.

Gratitude, Laughter, Divine

Think about today, and answer these questions in your journal:

- What are you grateful for today?
- What made you laugh today?
- Did you feel the Divine today?

Chapter 10
Leg 8: Late September 2019

Gary Shares: "I have the awareness, the ability, and the willingness to recreate myself."

I arrived back home in Washington on September 18th. Hera had grown so much while I was in Europe! It took several days to recover from jet lag, and I stopped journaling every day. I got lost in my tiredness, was not doing my inner work, and began fretting about all the things I could not control, which made me angry. Very quickly, my body exhibited the energy of anger, created by my angry thoughts, in the form of a UTI (urinary tract infection). How appropriate, my thoughts were about being "pissed off," and my body's response was to mirror being pissed off in a very physical way. If you've never felt the pain of a UTI, I hope you never do. It's a very physical example of angry energy leaving the body. My body had to get rid of it somehow, and in this way, it was a painful clue about my negative thinking. I thanked my body for the reminder and took steps both medically and spiritually to let my anger go. I was grateful for the awareness, again coming more quickly, as my health and well-being were at stake.

The UTI was a timely reminder of the power of manifesting, good or not. It got me thinking about another time where I used the powers of manifestation for good. I submitted my chapter for the next collaborative book with my publisher, *Manifestations: True Stories of Bringing the*

Imagined into Reality. I wrote about how a few years ago, I created abundance by focusing during a group meditation, not on my financial troubles, but instead on abundance for everyone in the room. Within two days and between two sources, over $22,000 unexpectedly flowed to me! I titled the chapter, *Altruistic Alchemy in Action* because in giving my energy to the whole, instead of just me, I opened the door for abundance to flow to me.

I flew to Jacksonville a few days later, excited to produce a grief retreat for widows. The day after I arrived, I spoke with a good friend who had gone through some challenges and was now on the other side of them. Her story confirmed that I made the right choice in putting my needs first and creating boundaries for what I would no longer accept in my life. We need to hear other people's stories of challenge and triumph so we can see that possibility is also there for us. We can't do this alone. In seeing her power, I took even more of mine back. In witnessing her taking control of her destiny, I saw that I could take control of mine, too. We mirror the examples of the brave souls we allow in our lives. By writing this book, I hope to be that same example to all who read my story. We free each other by inspirational example, and thus, we free ourselves even more.

Our widow's grief retreat began on a Friday evening at the beautiful Hyatt Regency on the St. John's River in downtown Jacksonville. Throughout the weekend, I had the honor of serving so many amazing ladies, all navigating through grief. It was a small production, and I had to run the AV! It was a bit nerve-wracking, but I did it. I was so proud of what we created!

I spent a couple days with my daughter, and on the last day of September, I returned to snow in Washington. September 30, 2019, would have been my and Gary's 22nd wedding anniversary. When we marry, the intent is to live the rest of our lives with the one we love. But sadly, only one of us gets to have that experience. He got to live the rest of his life with me! I didn't get to live the rest of my life with him. I'm honored that I made that happen for him.

Flashback: October 2017-January 2018

Once Gary came home from the hospital, the challenge was to manage everything that needed to be done to maintain his health after the surgeries.

We got into the rhythm of his feedings, including all the different medications he needed. My alarm sounded every three hours. I would arise and prepare everything. All the medications went through the feeding tube, either added by liquid or pills that we crushed with a mortar and pestle. It was challenging and very tiring. I remember thinking that it was like when my kids were babies, and I was nursing them. I got little sleep, was tired and frustrated, and it was so hard. Gary felt like he wasn't in control of anything and totally dependent on me for everything. We started getting short with each other and arguing, even not speaking to each other at times.

One day I came home from work, and Gary was so proud of himself. He had created a contraption where he could feed himself! He took a foot-long piece of wood that was an inch wide and attached some heavy wire that he bent into shape to hold the syringe tube in place. He placed the wood into the side of the couch, between the arm and the cushion, and then he was free to use both hands to feed himself. This genius invention allowed him to have some control over his illness, which made all the difference for him. The only hiccup was that occasionally the connections would come apart, and it would make a mess, which was super frustrating when it happened. He sure would cuss up a storm!

We also had to get used to packing everything up if we wanted to go shopping or spend the day out of the house. We had a bag always at the ready so that Gary felt like he could still live life and not be stuck at home. Occasionally, as at home, messes would happen in the car, and the cussing would commence, but at least we were able to get out of the house.

The second big challenge was keeping his trach clean and clear. There were times I had to use a tweezer to remove skin and scabs around the stoma. Oftentimes, we had to squirt saline into the stoma so that he could cough out phlegm. This was scary because it was blocking his airway. Several times a day, the trach tube would need to be removed to clear out mucus, then be cleaned, sterilized, and put back in. Because of the tender skin around the stoma, it was painful. The tumor began to grow on the outside of his neck and was now about the size of a golf ball. Every time I cleaned his trach, I took off the tumor dressing, applied the cream, and redressed it. Then I attached the trach collar to the trach tube and reinserted it.

One moment that was heartbreaking to see was Gary looking in the mirror, with the horrible tumor exposed and the trach tube out. He looked at me, with his hands first pointing to his neck, then up in the air in frustration, with the question in his eyes: How did this happen?

He continued to have his weekly chemo sessions after the surgeries. We would go to the oncology clinic once or twice a week, depending on his treatment schedule. On the chemo days, it took nearly a full day, and he usually fell asleep. Each session, they would insert the IV needle, which got harder each time as his veins began to collapse. Sometimes I would sit with him and read, but usually, he sent me off to do something for me.

Around mid-October, the oncologist was able to approve immunotherapy treatments. We were excited about the possibility of what that might do for his healing. The first week was fairly good, but as we rolled into the second and third weeks, his immune system just went wild, and it was exceedingly difficult for him. It was apparent that the immunotherapy was not working, so they canceled the treatment and put him back on chemo. That was very disheartening.

Because of his compromised veins, they put in a Groshong catheter that was attached to his chest on the left side. This was an easier way to administer the chemo treatments. Things went well for a while, but they determined that the chemo wasn't working well on its own anymore. They recommended adding radiation therapy. Gary wasn't thrilled. I think he agreed for my sake, although I never asked him to. He wanted to extend whatever time we had left, if even just a little bit.

On my birthday in November, Gary wanted to do something special for me. We made the two-hour drive to Portland, Oregon. We had always loved going to Portland to shop, eat at great restaurants, and walk around the city. Our favorite area was NW 23rd Avenue, with so many amazing shops and cafes. We stayed at the Marriott on the Willamette River and had the best time, even with Gary in the condition he was in. I was so grateful that he was able to go out with me and celebrate.

For Thanksgiving, Gary made me a great meal. It was wonderful to watch him in his element as he cooked a wonderful Thanksgiving dinner for one while creating an enduring memory for two.

For Christmas, I flew the kids home because I intuitively felt this might be our last Christmas together. We had a nice celebration, and I'll always cherish the special pictures of all of us together, even though Gary was not looking well at all. The smile on his face was all I needed to show me that this was a perfect final holiday for him.

As 2018 rolled in, I don't think either of us really knew what was coming. Or, at least, we kept it out of our minds. The combination of the chemo and the radiation was so hard on his body, and he started to decline rapidly. One day in January, we were sitting in our living room upstairs, and he got up to walk to the bathroom. Suddenly, I heard a big thud, and I found him on the floor, his eyes wide open and obviously unconscious. He came to quickly and insisted he was fine. I called the ambulance anyway, and they came and took him to the hospital as I followed behind. He was experiencing abdominal pain, dizziness, severe anemia, and exceptionally low blood pressure. He was given two units of blood.

What Are The Gifts?

We can still travel, even when we are compromised. The human body is so resilient, even when it's terribly ill. When the mind insists, like Gary wanting to take me to Portland for my birthday, the body musters up its reserves and delivers. Through Gary's experience after the surgeries and learning to live within cancer's limits, he showed me that life is still worth living. Every time I get sad or angry, I think of Gary's resilient spirit that rose above the glaring truth of his human condition. If he can find joy and purpose in life, with a body nearly defeated by cancer, I can find it within myself to rise out of the ashes of grief to find joy and purpose too. That's what he expects of me! And now, it's what I expect of myself.

Activity: Creating Magic

- What if you could do anything you wanted? What would it be?
- What three actions can you take to make it happen?
- How would you feel as you were completing these actions?
- How would you feel once you created what you desired?
- Journal about it for 15 minutes, and then read this entry every day for the next 21 days, as that's how long it takes to map in a new habit.
- Take at least one of your three actions today!

Gratitude, Laughter, Divine

Think about today, and answer these questions in your journal:

- What are you grateful for today?
- What made you laugh today?
- Did you feel the Divine today?

Chapter 11
Leg 9: October-November 2019

Gary Shares: "I am kind to all people that I encounter. I am engaged in activities that help the world."

O n October 3, 2019, I left for Australia for six weeks. I spent the first few days on the Sunshine Coast. The sounds of birds, insects, and who knows what else were so amazing. I went on a whale-watching trip, mesmerized by a momma whale teaching her baby to play, breach, jump, and smack its tail and fins. Such majestic creatures.

A few days later, I was on my way to Melbourne to stay with my amazing host and beloved friend. She lovingly invited me into her wonderful haven and created a safe space where I could rest and heal. I especially enjoyed the youthful company of her two beautiful granddaughters. Her two pets were also great companions, Jazzy the dog and Sassy the cat, a gorgeous gray creature with alluring green eyes.

Sitting on the Yarra River in Melbourne on a lovely spring day, I thought about what a great life I have! Grateful for my freedom and the ability to travel when I want and wherever I want. Proud that I created this life. I chose this. Good for me.

We went to the National Gallery to see the Terracotta Warriors, which were discovered in China in 1974 when local farmers were digging an irrigation well. They were created by Emperor Qin Shihuang as part of his quest for immortality.

Another living artist was featured alongside the warriors. He had an amazing display of terracotta birds hanging from the ceiling in flight. Standing below hundreds of them was like witnessing murmuration in stillness. Mesmerizing and breathtaking.

There were huge murals of peonies called Transience. I learned that peonies in full bloom have been an important motif in Chinese art for centuries. They symbolize royalty, virtue, honor, and wealth. Two works in this gallery were by Cai Guo-Qiang, gunpowder drawing on silk, depicting the peony's four-stage life cycle: emergence of the bud, blooming, wilting, and decaying. I loved his profound explanation: *I never thought I would be so moved by the decline of flowers; their withering is no less than the soul departing the body! Sometimes I wonder if life is merely an illusion, a dream, and that the soul actually manifests upon dying, which is the origin and the eternal state of things. Yet death is more elusive, more complex than that.*

These words really touched me, given Gary's death and the fact that peonies are my favorite flower. I have four peony bushes at home in Gary's gardens. As Gary's body withered away, he was beginning to feel more connected to Spirit. I intuitively knew that I was losing him to his Spirit, to his higher self. I knew that through all the pain of withering, he was enduring it longer than he needed to, and the reason for that was me. When I knew there was no miracle coming, I told him I would be okay, that he didn't need to worry about me anymore, he was free to go on his next journey.

When the peony is at its best, it is one of the most beautiful flowers, and many have a heavenly scent. When it begins to fade, you see it very slightly as the outer petals begin to drop off. Many of the petals will hold on for dear life, and only when they are moved do the petals instantly fall off, like it's holding itself in suspended animation to maintain its existence to experience the beauty of life just one more day. And that was exactly what Gary was doing, hanging on and enduring the pain for just one more day of our life together. I didn't realize it then as I read that at the museum, yet I instinctively took a picture. As I read it again now as I'm writing this book, I totally get the connection. I couldn't have taken the message in then, as I wasn't ready for it. Nine months later, I now understood.

We visited a garden in Jindivick that my friend had been wanting to visit. As we drove up, we were greeted by a bright orange sign saying *May Peace Prevail on Earth*, and behind it was a majestic landscape. This part of Australia reminds me of the Pacific Northwest, with all its many shades of green.

In the gardens, we met some beautiful peacocks, the usual colorful ones and a pure white one. We ventured to the back of the gardens where the owners lived. There were columns all along the back of the house, with wisteria draping the structure so elegantly. The garden was huge and meandering and so beautifully created and maintained. The owners designed and created it themselves over the years and decided to share its beauty with the public. There were many kinds of flowers and trees, some that I had seen in the US, but many that were totally new for me. It was like walking into a completely new world with so many new shapes and colors to experience. The gardens were accented by many sculptures and metal art pieces that were meticulously placed for maximum beauty and enjoyment. Many of the bushes were trimmed into shapes and creations, reminding me of the gardens at Versailles in France.

One day, I hung out with the alpacas and the lone sheep. The alpacas were such curious animals and so adorable with their bobbleheads and big eyes. I visited Gary's tree, which my friend had planted in one of her paddocks in honor of him after he passed. Gary was able to meet her twice, once in Australia and again in Cancun, Mexico, and they became fast friends. It was so humbling to visit the tree, to know that she honored him just as I had. She had planted another tree at the same time, and Gary's was outgrowing that one. I guess he likes his Australian tree!

I had a dream one morning that Gary was still alive and left me for an old girlfriend. I was so angry because I couldn't talk to him and then I woke up. The pain was so heavy because he was alive, and I couldn't have him. I came back to reality and remembered he's dead. In that moment, I didn't know which pain was harder: being left while he's alive or being left while he's dead. When alive, there's the constant reminder that he's alive and not with you, and there's nothing you can do. When dead, there's the constant reminder that he's dead and not with you, and there's nothing you can do. At least when alive, there's a small hope that he'll come back. But that small hope can be dashed countless times, over many years, and dim your light. It's not a contest. They are both heavy lessons of loss. And the only way through is moving forward and taking action. Phew! It was tough reliving that again!

Just about every day, I walked and either listened to nature or an audiobook. One day, walking along the rural highway, I got a sign from Spirit. I came upon a wooden block inscribed with the name Sarah. The meaning of Sarah is lady, princess, or noblewoman. I guess Spirit is telling me that I must treat myself like a princess! I come first and deserve to be loved and honored, especially by me! Thank you, Spirit, for reminding me!

On another walk, I found three beautiful feathers, one black, one gray, and the third was black and white. I went to the bathroom at the park and set them on the sink on a piece of toilet paper. There was no wind inside, yet they were gone when I finished! Not on the ground, not outside, it was like they vanished into thin air! I like to think that Gary left those feathers for me and then took them back laughing as I looked all around the rustic bathroom, knowing how I disliked bathrooms like this!

A few days later, we drove to Dromana Beach for a girls' weekend with two other lovely ladies. I had a great time with my three Ozzie girls, grateful for the beach walks, heart-to-heart talks, winery tours, and collecting trinkets from the sea—heart and butterfly-shaped shells and spirals like Gary used to find! The water was beautiful turquoise green as we passed the colorful beach huts.

Life is meant to live, to experience love in people. My best meditations are when I'm fully alive, aware, and present with life, out in nature, walking on a beautiful beach, finding treasures from the sea. Having a friend walking with me is heaven. Enjoying a nice cup of tea and engaging in interesting conversation is a beautiful meditation of being present with people you love. Those are heavenly gifts I give to myself, gifts that could never be experienced behind an eye mask in the dark. We are meant to take what we learn from those silent, contemplative meditations behind the mask to learn to manage our energy and then move out into the world with that heavenly energy and create joy, love, and compassion. Support everyone's highest good and allow for our highest voice to be heard! That's a heavenly expression!

A few days after my son's birthday, I found out that his two older huskies, Zeus and Xena, had been missing since his birthday. I was saddened for my son, yet inspired by Jazzy, even though her health was failing. On this day, she was walking around and resting in the garden, barking, and seeming to enjoy nature. This trip would be the last time I would see Jazzy. I had seen her over the years on my trips to Australia, and she was such a beautiful presence. We never did find my son's dogs, and I hope they are with Jazzy.

I experienced many animals on my walks: cows, horses, donkeys, kookaburra, and many varieties of birds. The most memorable was a duck that walked ahead of me on the road for several minutes, sometimes waddling slowly and sometimes extremely fast. Once, he took flight, and I thought he was leaving, but he landed back on the road and kept walking. Somehow, I felt as if he were enjoying leading me on his walk. Finally, a car came toward us, and he flew off. They were sweet moments where all my attention was focused on this cute being, which reminded me about the importance and enjoyment of being present.

Next, I spent several minutes watching a flock of birds flying in formation. Every so often, they appeared to be in chaos, all flying in different directions as if something interrupted their focus and momentarily knocked them out of balance. Then quickly, they reformed and refocused on the whole and were immediately back in coherence. Reminded me of my journey through grief, with some days calm and some days chaotic, but ultimately, I can still regroup, refocus, and live my life in joy.

Later in the day, we went to visit some friends in Millgrove. It was a wonderful time of reminiscing, laughing, and remembering the good times we had with those who had departed this world in the last years: one in July 2017, another in February 2018, and Gary in June 2018. Such amazing and inspirational humans who had graced us with their presence and taught us so much about tenacity, resilience, grace, and dignity.

It was springtime in Australia, and my friend's garden was ablaze in floral beauty. From the snowball bushes to the poppies, wisteria, and calla lilies, and finally the roses and bougainvillea.

We went into town often and had coffee with my friend's older granddaughter. Her favorite "coffee" drink she dubbed a Baby Chornay, always with two marshmallows and sprinkles. When she was done, and she always finished it, she had a cute chocolate mustache! I enjoyed her youthful zeal, and I especially loved watching her brush Jazzy with water from her water bowl. Such a compassionate experience to witness. We took a walk together one day around the yard, and we tied little yellow and white daisies to her sandals. Such a sweet time with her, seeing life through the eyes of a curious child. It was so good for my grieving heart!

We spent a few days in Melbourne, attending a workshop and visiting with friends. A surprise hot air balloon trip was on the agenda for my birthday! We began at 5 a.m., prepping for a 6 a.m. takeoff from Footscray Park. Three balloons followed our red and white Nova balloon. One was a bright yellow balloon for Yellowtail Winery; a lavender one for Nudie, creators of good; and finally, a red and gray one for Fox 101.9. There were ten of us in the basket with the pilot. When the flames were on above us, it was hot and sounded like putting air in your tires. The morning was a little chilly, so the flames were a nice heater to keep us comfortable. We flew over Lynch's Bridge, Newell's Paddock, and a Buddhist Temple with graffiti on its walls. As the sun rose beautifully over West Melbourne, we sailed over the Ferris wheel, the Docklands, and Melbourne CBD (that's the central business district, not marijuana!). Next came the Treasury Gardens—a park that had been planted with trees to look like the Union Jack, and Fitzroy Gardens with a majestic cathedral with three spires. Finally, we flew over East Melbourne and some amazing rooftop gardens and on to a smooth landing at Burnley Oval.

Our next adventure was to the Royal Botanic Gardens for an aboriginal tour. We had an amazing guide who shared with us how they used plants. As we walked along, he was burning different plants and leaves in a wooden bowl. At the end, he created a fire in a bigger wooden bowl using what he had been burning on our walk. We each chose a leaf to put into the fire with our intentions and wishes. He shared a map of the indigenous cultures in Australia with us, and I learned there were over five hundred aboriginal clans.

Back at my friend's place, I was entertained watching and filming her cutting the grass in the paddock where Gary's tree was. She looked like a rebel riding that lawnmower, fast and furious past her two alpaca neighbors who watched her curiously. It was fun to see her man-handle this machine and know exactly how close she could get to the fence before throwing it into reverse. She then expertly opened the gate while still in motion, mowing the grass past the gate and then, with one strong push, she closed the gate and expertly moved the mower close to the gate to push it and latch it closed. Then she was done and off riding past Gary's tree and out of sight.

We were invited back to the nursery in Jindivick, where they were hosting a Peace Pole ceremony. The hole was dug, and the pole was in place. We were led in a ceremony by a representative from Japan and a local woman. We each grabbed a small rock and took turns putting our rocks, along with a small note of our written intentions, into the hole. When that was complete, we each put a shovel of dirt in. A prayer closed the ceremony. The pole had *May Peace Prevail on Earth* on its four sides in English, Japanese, Spanish, and French. These poles are placed worldwide with similar ceremonies. We then took a walk through the gardens, followed by a delicious lunch with many wonderful people. I was so grateful to be included in this ceremony.

I had eight days left, and I was anxious to get home. I had one of the strangest dreams. Gary was still alive, awfully close to death. He kept falling, and his hand fell off, and he reattached it. I was watching him from upstairs. He was in the kitchen with the drawer by the sink open. He said he found a rare coin in there and was soaking it in a jar of water. At one point, I hugged him and was crying. I said, "I'm only 54. What am I supposed to do with the rest of my life?"

We went back to Melbourne for the Australian Bush Flower Workshop. I stayed longer than I originally planned so I could attend this! Just outside the meeting room was a display case with crocheted poppies made by community members in celebration of Remembrance Day on November 11th. A beautiful poem read:

They shall not grow old,

As we that are left grow old.

Age shall not weary them,

Nor the years condemn.

At the going down of the sun and in the morning,

We will remember them.

Our good friend Doug came over for dinner, and we decided to hold a ceremony for Gary at his tree. We had dried flowers already prepared in a bowl, and we began an impromptu trek through the garden to pick some fresh flowers for our ceremony. Doug collected the flowers in a larger bowl, and then we set a tall candle holder with cutouts for the light to shine through under Gary's tree. There was a bright shining moon out at 10:16 p.m. We placed all the flowers around the tree, said a few words in his honor, and raised our wine glasses to toast him. Sassy joined us for the festivities. The next morning it was raining hard and continued to rain hard well past 10:25 a.m. The candle was still burning over twelve hours later, even amidst heavy rains! Thank you, Gary, for keeping your light burning. Thank you to my beautiful friends for sharing the ceremony with me and for my gracious host for planting the tree. Several months later, we lost Doug unexpectedly, so it was almost as if this ceremony was for him, too. I'm sure he and Gary are having fun on the other side!

It's November 12th, my 56th birthday! My friend treated me to a facial, and then we went to Melbourne for the day. We walked through Federation Square and toured an aboriginal museum. We had yummy Asian food for lunch. I knew we were having dinner in the city, but I was surprised with several friends joining us to celebrate at Café Guillaume. So grateful and blessed to celebrate this second birthday after Gary's passing with my Aussie friends who loved him!

Days later, I took a selfie of myself and sent it to one of the friends on our girls' beach trip. One of the things we had each promised was that we were going to learn new things. This friend committed to learning how to weave on her Mother's loom that her Father had made for her. At my birthday dinner, she had presented me with her first project on that loom, a gorgeous scarf. I was so honored!

One day we went on a little road trip to Stoney Creek to pick up a garden sculpture that I bought for my friend, to thank her for her love and care. We stopped for lunch in Mirboo North at a cute cafe. On the wall were all kinds of magazine cutouts pasted to the wall. One that was especially poignant for me said: *Sometimes you have to be away to appreciate home. Having lived abroad for a number of years, I travel to my hometown for the holidays, and suddenly, naturally, Gippsland turned on her charm.*

The sculpture was so cool! We had seen it at a garden show a few weeks earlier, and my friend just loved it. It was created by an older gentleman who welded metal farm stuff into works of art. The base was a large triangle metal piece, most likely from a large farming machine. There were six horseshoes around the triangle, one on each corner and one between each corner. The open ends of the horseshoes were welded to the triangle base so that it looked like a flower with petals. In the center of the triangle was a metal tube where a curved metal piece slotted into. The curved piece looked like it was made from wagon wheels. At the top of the curved piece hung a short metal chain, from which a large globe hung suspended, which was made of barbed wire. She later placed it next to Gary's tree!

November 14th was my last day in Australia. I was ready to go home but sad to leave such a precious friend who had taken such great care of me. I'm forever grateful to her for putting up with me for so long. I took one last walk around the serene gardens and visited the animals: Jazzy, Sassy, the alpacas, the lone sheep, and finally Gary's tree, as I wanted to remember them all on this perfect day.

I arrived in Seattle on the same day I left Australia! As I arrived home to my and Gary's house after nine months of traveling, I truly felt at peace here. Gary's energy was all around, his handiwork was all around, yet the place was now my own to grow and thrive in.

Flashback: February-March 2018

A dear friend of ours died in February 2018 from cancer. She decided to end treatment and then stopped eating. At first, I did not share with Gary about her not eating, as I was afraid he would consider doing the same. When the time of his death came closer, he spoke to the doctors about compassionate death, and they said he would need two doctors to approve the fatal dose of medication. Or he could just stop eating. I then shared about our friend choosing this option and assured him that she did not suffer.

When he asked a psychic friend for guidance, she told him Spirit said he had healed himself in so many lifetimes that he'd mastered healing. Now it was time to move on. He resigned himself to the fact that he was not going to pull off another miracle. When Gary's pain became totally debilitating, I told him I wanted him to be free and happy. He had suffered enough.

In March, Gary was back in the hospital. He was not doing well and had to have another blood transfusion. The site where the catheter was inserted in his chest had started to ooze green, and they determined he had a staph infection. When they removed the catheter, he did not get any kind of pain medication. They just pulled it out, like ripping off a bandage, and it was one of the most painful things he endured during that stay. We were in the hospital for a few more days while they got the infection under control. Finally, they set him up with a permanent IV in his arm for his chemo treatments.

At this point, we called our attorney, and she came to the hospital to sign the power of attorney papers. She recommended that we check with his former employer to see if there were any life insurance policies in place. We told her we didn't think there were, but she recommended we check anyway. When we got home a couple days later, I found out there was, in fact, a life insurance policy that would pay a small but still significant amount! We didn't have a life insurance policy for Gary, and we were so grateful for this unexpected gift given the circumstances.

What Are The Gifts?

Sometimes we just have to let go and allow God to take the reins. In surrendering with love and trust, we open ourselves to a peaceful place of acceptance and gratitude. When we can see the gifts that every experience provides, whether tragedy or triumph, we become aware of the infinite goodness that surrounds us. Every experience offers a nugget of wisdom if we choose to see it. Spirit offers us whispers of love if we choose to hear them. Unexpected gifts, like the life insurance, are proof that a higher power is always looking out for our highest good.

I have taken this way of looking at life, being grateful for every experience with me as I traveled. If Gary can surrender to love, I can too.

Activity: Serving Others

- What would be your ultimate way of being of service? People, nature, volunteer, donate? Choose two.
- Do some Google research on how or where you can do this. Make contact and get the ball rolling.
- Ask Spirit to be of service.
- If you are dealing with death, what can you do now to honor your loved one that will serve others?
- If you are dealing with a challenging situation, how can you use that experience to serve others?

Gratitude, Laughter, Divine

Think about today, and answer these questions in your journal:

- What are you grateful for today?
- What made you laugh today?
- Did you feel the Divine today?

Chapter 12
Leg 10: November 2019-
February 2020

Gary Shares: "My challenges are now my gifts. I forgive myself for taking so long."

It's been three days since arriving back home from Australia. I've slept a lot! The jet lag is a doozy!

I decided to get another tattoo in honor of Gary. I had gotten one years earlier on my 42nd birthday as a gift from Gary, a small lotus flower near my right shoulder. I had grand plans of adding onto it down the road, which I quickly scrapped before it was even done. It was so painful! The outlining in black ink wasn't so bad, feeling like mild electric shocks. Filling in the colors was truly painful. It felt like wiping over severely sunburned skin. I vowed I was done with tattoos! But then, a few days ago, I saw a picture of a tattoo on Facebook that replicated a departed loved one's handwriting. Gary had beautiful handwriting, which would be ideal. Over the years, Gary had given me beautifully written cards for all the holidays and birthdays and also some just because. I went through all his cards and found the perfect one: *As near as a thought...remember I love you. Gary*

What I love about this is that it could be interpreted three ways:

1. Gary saying it to me
2. Me saying it to Gary
3. God saying it to Gary

On November 27th, I had it tattooed on the inside of my right arm just below the elbow, where I could easily see it. I also added a hummingbird. I endured the electric shock treatment in honor of Gary, and who knows, maybe someday I will add color to the hummingbird!

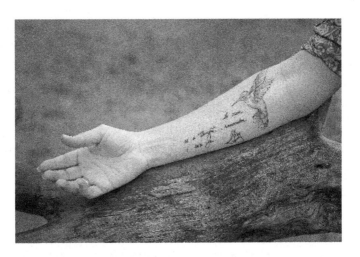

On a cool, misty day, I ventured to Seattle and visited Green Lake Park. As I was walking around the lake, I met another heron. It was standing on a log just off the shore, almost as if it were waiting for me. What a beauty it was! He had a gray hombre pattern to his feathers, lighter at the top and darker at the bottom. These colors were offset by a yellow beak. His long legs ended with big prehistoric-looking claws.

I happened upon a large rock, one that Gary would have loved to have in our yard. As I walked up to it, I noticed it had a little plaque on it which said: *ODO '71, "Rock on..."* Later, I did some research on this rock, and it's a mystery who placed it there and what the plaque means. Perhaps ODO are the initials of someone who died in 1971? Jim Morrison died in 1971. So did the original Shamu. I laughed to think that perhaps the Rock Gods are messing with us!

My mom arrived in town to support me during my eye surgeries. I was having refractive lensectomies in both eyes. That's where they take out my natural lenses and replace them with an artificial lens. It would get me back to 20/20 vision, and I would only need reading glasses for very close-up work. I was a bit nervous about the procedure, but a friend of mine had it done many years ago and highly recommended it.

I had perfect vision up until around the time I got an iPhone 3. The iPhone was such a great device to use for my work, and I was soon addicted to it. Along with constantly working on a laptop, I believe this was the turning point for my vision. I basically had to wear glasses all the time. It was fun at first to find stylish glasses. Over the years, I've probably had about a dozen cool pairs. As time passed, I got tired of not being able to wear sunglasses while driving or while reading on the beach. I had to constantly consider what activities to do related to my glasses. And continually misplacing them.

The procedure was quick and simple. I had my right eye done first, and then a week later, the left. The only pain I experienced was the drops to ward off infection. Those stung like crazy! I'm so happy that I had this done and am no longer dependent on glasses. It's wonderful to be free to see again with my bionic eyes!

One day, after one of my follow-up appointments, we stopped and had donuts in Tacoma on 6th Ave. Gary and I had donuts here once, on a day we chose to explore Tacoma. We often would take day trips and visit areas we hadn't been to and try out new places to eat. The donuts were huge and very decadent. I had a caramel donut, and mom had the Snickers!

With Christmas fast approaching, mom and I took an excursion in search of small-town holiday spirit. We had no plans, just to head west and see what we could find. We drove up Hwy 101 near Evergreen State College, and on the way, we saw a small group of bald eagles in the evergreen trees.

In Shelton, we came across a Christmas maze, guarded by the lumberjack Paul Bunyan and Babe the Blue Ox. The maze was made of Christmas trees in planter boxes, all lit up with white lights. We had fun winding our way through the maze, as jubilant kids were also finding their way through, going in the opposite direction. At the end of the maze, we walked through a red and gold archway and got up close and personal with the huge Paul Bunyan. We laughed as we realized he looked just like Burt Reynolds!

Our next holiday excursion was to head north to Pike Place Market in Seattle. The Christmas lights were beautiful.

I had never been to the market for the holidays. We got a beautiful bouquet of flowers, which are always available at the market and a must buy anytime I go. There were throngs of people everywhere, dressed up in Santa costumes, holiday business suits, and elf costumes. It was the big holiday event, SantaCon, held in cities around the world. It's basically a Santa convention, where everyone dresses up like Santa. I love the answer to why SantaCon: *Because it's fun. That is all. It's one of the few chances left for adults to be silly without any kind of agenda.*

In the evening, we went to a small concert at a church, Navidad, by Pacific Musicworks. I thought it was going to be more ethnic and vibrant due to the title and the pictures promoting it, but we still enjoyed the beautiful music performed by the musicians and singers. We also got to experience a neighborhood I'd never been to and see all the houses lit up so beautifully for the holidays.

I enjoyed sharing these times with my mom. I thanked Gary for having shared many excursions like this in the past.

One morning at 11:15, the sun was shining brightly through the skylight as I was sitting in my living room upstairs. I took several pictures of the sunlight coming through. The picture taken at 11:19 has a heart-shaped halo around the top of the skylight. It also looked like a kaleidoscope with many vibrant colors, along with white and gold light emanating from the top right and the bottom left. I was taking the picture from the spot where Gary died. It felt like a gorgeous display of love and peace!

Later in the afternoon, we headed into Yelm for a basket weaving class. Mom was much more patient with the process than I was, and she had to help me out when I got frustrated! It was amazing how pliable the wet wooden strips were as we wove our creations. Our baskets turned out beautifully. Mom's had a band of purple around it, while mine had a band of turquoise. Hers was more open at the top and even with the base. Mine was narrower at the top because as I was getting a bit frustrated, I started weaving it tighter at the top. Funny how making baskets mimics our mindset! It was still super cute and now holds treasures on my bookcase!

On another day trip to Tacoma, we found this sign: *Sometimes you don't get closure, you just move on.* There are so many times in our lives when big things happen, and little things happen. No matter the size, big or little, they can have a major impact on our lives and create blocks that keep us from moving forward. We don't always get closure, and that's okay. When we don't get closure, there is a reason for that, a lesson that we need to learn, usually about resilience.

On December 20th, I received my angel and word for 2020 from my spiritual mentor. This was a new experience for me. My angel was Charmiene, the Angel of Harmony (boy, would I need her in 2020!) She helps to attain harmony through self-love, and an important aspect is to feel what it feels like to be me, to have courage and face my fears. I found a gorgeous picture of Charmiene and created an image with her name and my word. I ordered a mouse pad and several postcards that I placed around my space. I couldn't have known that 2020 would also bring the grief of the pandemic, racial unrest, and a crazy election year. My word was Creator, and I would surely need the energy of creation to navigate all the changes 2020 would bring to my professional life. As I look back, now at the end of 2020, I'm so grateful for this guidance that helped to sustain and ground me through a tumultuous year.

We celebrated Christmas 2019 with a yummy dinner, love from friends and family, and memories of past Christmases with Gary. Mom made a great prime rib dinner. My job was the prep cook and cleanup, just like I used to do with Gary. We had a nice quiet Christmas, no gifts, no tree, only two centerpieces, two wreaths, and a purple poinsettia! Simplicity!

Another day trip to Seattle found us on the Great Wheel at Pier 57. We had car number 32 all to ourselves. Mom was a little uncomfortable, and of course, they stopped us at the very top for several minutes while they loaded people below. We had a fantastic view of the sound, with the loading docks, the city, the Seahawks and Mariners Stadiums, and the ferries coming in. We also got to see two tugboats bringing in a ship full of shipping containers.

Of course, we had to stop by Pike Place Market again! We walked by the Seattle Art Museum and saw the big Hammer Man Statue in front of the museum. Someone had crocheted ankle bracelets around his foot. Around Seattle and Tacoma, you see bike racks and street signs with crocheted coverings. And my mom is a crocheter, so she especially appreciated them.

When doubt creeps in, rather than let it take hold, I thank it for reminding me of the amazing life I'm creating. That being big means being challenged. And the goal is to move beyond the challenge into new territory, where the magic is!

I woke up two times the night of December 30th smelling Gary's cologne! Mom also was woken up around 2:30 a.m., thinking she heard a cat in her room. Hello Gary!

It's the final day of December 2019, and I'm thinking about all I'm grateful for, the lessons of 2019, and the magic to come in 2020. I'm also reminded that 2018 was my last year with Gary in it. 2019 my last year with my job in it. 2020 will be my first year with the new me!

Happy New Year! A new year, a new decade, the roaring 20s! I started my day on January 1, 2020, being committed to doing my work, taking care of me, and revamping my calendar. And a new class with my teacher, I Choose Me 2020!

January 2nd was the one-year anniversary of resigning from my job. A whole year has gone by. It's been a difficult struggle, making the transition out of the group and people falling away. I'm grateful for the lesson of believing in myself no matter what, and for those continuing to stand by and support me. Reminding me that I am visible. That my voice is important and deserves to be heard. Especially that I matter! These are just lessons for me to learn and grow from, and to learn how to treat others respectfully. This is my year to create a magical life with the right people. They will show up! I love my life and what I'm creating!

I woke up one morning from a bad dream where a former colleague was influencing my future, and I slept through my class. I was so upset about the dream and missing class. I listened to the recording as soon as it was available, and the topic was the importance of managing our energy and invoking Archangel Michael to help with that. It was just what I needed to change my attitude and energy. I realized I had absorbed the bad energy from my dream and carried it into my day. Getting centered and asking Archangel Michael to help showed me that I can do this, that I'm connected to Spirit always and in an instant!

Another morning I awoke from another weird dream. I think Gary was with me in the beginning. We went to a party at a friend's house, in a strange place like an amusement park. We were hiding from my friend the entire time. At one point, my friend came into the room I was in, and I wasn't sure if I was seen. Then I was outside of the home, lost my phone, and trying to find a taxi to leave. When I awoke, I immediately called in Archangel Michael and felt at peace and safe.

Dreams are just ways our fears show up. I don't need to hide from anyone. I deserve to stand tall and proud in my own way. I took this energy into organizing my office today. I allowed a good flow of love and wealth to come in.

Every day I ask God, angels, guides, and loved ones to help me put the past behind me, so it's not part of my present anymore. And I allow them to be wise reminders of a past learning experience that served me well!

Last night I had another weird dream about Gary. He was very unstable, and we couldn't find him. He then showed up at our house, not the one I live in now, and held a rifle to my face. He was sitting on a shelf on the second floor, with the lower floor beneath him, which shouldn't have supported his weight. Very weird. Someone was with me, a young man, but not my son. As I thought about this dream, it came to me that it wasn't about Gary's actions in the dream. It was about the guilt I felt for feeling like I failed him as a caregiver. In that moment, I gave myself grace and benevolence, knowing that I did the best I could in those circumstances. I was reminded of the psychic reading where Gary thanked me for all I did for him.

I'm back in Denver, and it's February 2, 2020. A palindrome date, the same forward as backward, 02022020. I laughed as I remembered my high school teacher, Mr. Heath, teaching us about palindromes. Mom and I are getting ready to go on the road again! I'm excited about new landscapes, friends, new people, and freedom!

A funny thing happened last night as I was leaving to meet my dad for dinner. I suggested to mom that I take the painting to him that our cousins, Alex and Anna, had gotten them in Spain many years ago when my parents were still together. Dad had once asked about it, but mom kept it. She was fine with me taking it and dusted it off, and found a nice bag to protect it. I put it in my truck. It had been snowing all day, so it was cold and icy. As I was backing out of the garage, the tires slid on the ice and lodged the truck against the garage doorway, half in and half out. There was no way to go forward or backward without damaging the truck. I called AAA, who arrived in about 20 minutes. He used his fancy tow truck to pull it sideways away from the wall. Thankfully, there were just some minor scratches. We parked the truck and mom's SUV back safely in. A while later, we remembered the painting was in the car, and mom went and got it. We laughed that Anna must've wanted the painting to stay with mom. Later, while watching Wheel of Fortune, the background scene had a picture of a street with some storefronts. One of the stores was Alex and Anna's!

150

We are keeping Anna's painting! We laughed that Anna created the truck getting stuck! No harm done, she got her wish, and we got the message!

Our February road trip took us to Santa Fe and Sedona, where we visited with good friends and did a site visit for an upcoming event. Then we drove to Algodones, Mexico, where we stayed for a week while I had dental work done. We finished our journey driving west to California and up the west coast, through Oregon, and finally to Washington. I hadn't journaled much on the road, but I posted my Day Tripper Challenge every day on Facebook. Gratitude, laughter, divine are everywhere!

Flashback: April-May 2018

Gary continued to do chemotherapy but stopped the radiation for a while because it was just debilitating his body. When we finally went back to the radiation oncologist on a Tuesday, he said he didn't think there was any more that could be done. The radiation wasn't doing anything and wasn't worth the effects on his body.

After we left the radiation oncologist, we were driving to our next appointment with the chemo oncologist. We both knew this was it. The silence was deafening. We pulled into the parking lot, and Gary said to me, *"I know you're supposed to go to Germany on Thursday, but I would really like for you to stay with me and help me transition. It's time."* We both broke down and cried. When it was time to go into our appointment, we met with the chemo oncologist, and he agreed there was nothing more to be done and referred us to hospice.

The ride home was a quiet ride. Neither of us said anything. We were just in our own minds, afraid to speak, knowing that our time was short, and just not sure what to say. I think both of us were afraid of breaking down, afraid that if we said anything, it would make it real and make it happen faster. We were afraid of running out of time. It was the strangest ride home. When we got home, Gary went to the couch and set himself up to get his feeding in, and I just sat with him. Neither of us saying a word. We just wanted to be in each other's energy and be near each other, knowing that very soon, the end would come.

In the last few weeks, as we discussed the things we needed to discuss and expressed our love and appreciation for our life together, I asked my husband to send me signs from the other side that he was okay. I promised to look for them.

Watching someone slowly die before your eyes is one of the most painful things to witness. Gary passed away on June 1, 2018, at 3:55 p.m. in our home. He didn't have much time to "age gracefully," in fact, the cancer made sure it wasn't graceful at all. At least, not physically. In the short time that was left, he showed me how to "age gratefully." When you can age gratefully, regardless of what your body shows you, what life shows you, or what your experiences show you, that is how you "age gracefully!"

Here are key lessons I learned watching Gary age prematurely and die at the young age of 62:

When he was diagnosed with throat cancer:

He did not wallow in pity or victimhood. Because of his 30+ years on his spiritual journey, he knew he was responsible for his body's illness. Instead, he looked within and determined what emotions caused his illness. He blessed and thanked the cancer for bringing this to his attention so that he could continue to evolve his thinking and being. He was a way-shower for me about the power of expression and what the consequences are when we choose not to express our voice out of fear or unworthiness.

He opted for non-traditional therapy that was still somewhat based on traditional methods. He understood that because of the severity of the cancer, he had to have one foot firmly planted in the modern medical world, while the other foot was anchored in the spiritual world. Even though he believed he had the power within to heal himself, he knew the best outcome for his highest good would require both worlds. And while the end result wasn't the healing he had hoped for, he was gifted with a little more time to learn what he needed to learn.

When it became clear that he was not going to live much longer:

He made the best of each day he had. He could have left it to me to handle all his feedings and medications, but he was independent to the end. He wanted to serve his body as best he could because he was so grateful for the service it had provided him throughout his life. In retrospect, he was consciously loving and honoring his body through the illness in a truly compassionate way.

He prepared cards and gifts for friends he was unable to see. His last act of love for me was having his brother send a card with an owl (my totem) for our anniversary that came a few months later. Rather than write the message for him, his brother included Gary's handwritten note. Such a graceful exit.

Memorial Day 2018 was bittersweet. Gary's family came, as the original plan was for them to stay with him while I went to Berlin. As a surprise, I flew our children in and invited other family and friends. Even though Gary was at his sickest, I knew inviting people into our home to celebrate him was important. He was mad at first. He didn't want to be remembered as a shell of the man he once was. But he quickly got over it. His energy severely sapped, he could visit only in short intervals, yet he kept coming outside to join us. One of the greatest gifts of his illness, he told me, was receiving so much love.

Our friends from Holland came to hold the space for Gary and me in his last week. Another friend connected with those waiting for him on the other side. She assured him they were ready to welcome him home whenever he was ready. Knowing that, and that so many people would love me in his place allowed Gary to make peace with dying.

Two days before he passed:

He awoke full of energy after being unconscious for a couple days. He tried to stand up and immediately fell as his legs could no longer support his emaciated body. He sustained some minor scratches and bruises, and when we got him back in his chair, he began speaking with the voice of a young teenage boy.

His first question was: "Is the tumor gone?" When I looked and said no, he matter-of-factly continued talking like it was no big deal.

I realized the power of Spirit when he stayed conscious in this younger version of himself, full of energy for the next 26 hours straight. He showed no signs of pain where the cancer was and fully moved that part of his body like it was completely healed.

He was constantly doing a ritual that looked like he was tying and untying things and stretching this "string" away from his body while looking at it with one eye, like he was assessing how best to apply it to whatever he was attaching it to. Then he performed another ritual with me and then his brother, where he had me put my hands together, like in prayer with the fingers pointing towards him, and then he tied these strings around my hands. As I questioned him about why he was doing this, I finally coaxed out of him that he was connecting us so that we would always be together.

His brother and I decided to take shifts while Gary was awake since he continued to try to stand up and move his electric chair. It was exhausting. It was the end of my shift, and I had moved his chair close to the couch so I could lie down. Earlier, Gary had insisted on going to the bathroom, so I helped him walk the short distance. It was hard work, as his legs were not strong. I got him back in his chair and tried to get him to rest for a bit. His brother arrived to take over, and I shared with him how my shift went. He got very frustrated with Gary and scolded him for not understanding how tired we were. The silence hung in the air for a few seconds, and then Gary very matter-of-factly said: *"Well, you don't have to be such an ass about it."* We laughed so hard! Gary didn't think it was funny. Apparently, he didn't appreciate being scolded by his younger brother. We would reminisce about this moment often after Gary passed. Another sweet moment was when I asked Gary if he knew who I was. He told me I was his girlfriend. I asked him if he knew who the man with us was. He said that was his big brother. I said, "He's your little brother." He replied, "But he's bigger than me."

I truly felt that these 26 hours were a gift from his Spirit, just for us. It was so amazing to be speaking to him in this way. A reminder of his youthful and energetic spirit and a comforting way of showing us that he IS Spirit and will always be with us. He wanted us to know that he was okay, that his body was simply a garment he used for this lifetime, which did not define his true spiritual nature.

What Are The Gifts?

I vowed I was not going to be a victim of his death. I was going to honor his life by living my life to the fullest, by surrounding myself with people who resonated with me and allowed me to grow and expand. Just as his Spirit grew and expanded despite the cancer and impending death, I would listen to my body with the promise to always honor the intuition it presented to me. Most importantly, I would not hide behind fear, grief, and loss. I would speak my truth for the highest good of all. As Gary's life set an inspirational example for me and others, I would endeavor every day to be an inspirational example as well. In his honor. And mine.

Activity: Story Time

- Be a light for others. Everyone has an inspiring story to share. What's yours?
- Write it down; it doesn't have to be long. Share it with one trusted person and ask for feedback.
- What were the 2 key lessons they got from reading your story?

Gratitude, Laughter, Divine

Think about today, and answer these questions in your journal:

- What are you grateful for today?
- What made you laugh today?
- Did you feel the Divine today?

Chapter 13
Leg 11: March-May 2020

Gary Shares: "Let it be now, in gratitude, I let it go and truly become the greatness of the true God that is within."

On March 3rd, I boarded a flight at SeaTac airport destined for Annapolis, Maryland. I spent a few blissful days with a wonderful couple I know, then took the train to New York City to attend the Women's Travel Fest conference. By then, we started to hear more about the Covid-19 virus. The event was still on, and honestly, I wasn't concerned about the virus. During the event, I stayed with a dear friend in her apartment in the city. It was within walking distance to the event, and I enjoyed this time to experience the city like a local. After the conference, I spent a few more days enjoying the company of my friends. The virus talk was heating up, and my friend had to cancel her trip to Italy, as that country was getting hit hard. No restrictions were in place yet in NYC, but you could feel the angst and fear rising.

One day, I did a site visit for a book launch party that was supposed to happen in May. My friend came with me, and we did some sightseeing. The site visit was near the Rockefeller Square Skating Rink, and the song, Another Day, by Paul McCartney was playing over the loudspeakers. Randomly, I remembered Paul's mother was named Mary. Nearby was Saint Patrick's Cathedral. We went inside, and at the back of the church, we saw the enclosed Mother Mary chapel. There was also a statue of Our Lady of Guadalupe.

I had met my friend many years ago at an event my previous employer held in Norwalk, Connecticut, about 45 miles from NYC. We reminisced about later events at the Carefree Resort in Arizona, and I shared with her that my contact there for all those years was named Mary. As we were walking back to the subway station, we passed a small church, Our Lady of Guadalupe. For some reason, Mother Mary was front and center on this day, and I was grateful for her presence.

The following day, I began my *Angels & Intuition* online course. I was happy that my intuition was increasing, and I was noticing more signs from the Divine every day. During the call, my pen stopped working. It was black ink. I grabbed a pen from my purse, and it was blue ink.

Later that day, I took an Uber to the airport, and the driver was wearing blue. There were beautiful blue skies as the flight took off. When we were having dinner, I was watching the David Crosby documentary, where he was talking about working with Jerry Garcia on an album. The flight attendant then brought me ice cream. It was Ben & Jerry's, the flavor was Cherry Garcia, and it was in a sky-blue container! The movie kept going out about every 30 minutes, and each time I would look out the window and see the beautiful blue hues of the sky after the sun had set. So surreal and breathtaking! Thank you, Spirit, for reminding me to see you in the simple things!

I arrived in Denver late in the evening on March 10th. The plan was to spend some time with my mom. I hadn't booked a flight home yet and planned to decide later. The pandemic began to hit hard in the US, as states started to lock down. Washington State, where the first case was reported to have happened, began lockdown. Colorado soon followed. I guess I wasn't going home just yet. I was grateful that I could be with my mom during this time so that she didn't have to experience this alone. Sheltering in place was fun at first. Reminded me of summer break after a long year of school.

As things began to escalate, my clients and I had to make backup plans for events that were coming up in the spring and summer. Some became virtual events. Some were rescheduled to 2021. Others were canceled. It was an unsettling time, especially as I was just starting my event planning business.

During one day of the *Angels & Intuition* course, we had automatic writing homework with Archangel Gabriel. Automatic writing is where you connect with Spirit and allow the words to come through you and write them down without thinking about them. We were instructed to start the exercise with this intention: I am open to receive all messages that Archangel Gabriel has to offer me. I began the exercise, and here is some of what I wrote:

Gabriel is similar to Gary's name in that it starts with GA. With Archangel Gabriel being the angel of comm-unication, it's fitting that he would remind me of Gary. Gary couldn't speak verbally at the end, and his illness was such a harsh experience to get the lesson about not having a voice.

We all have a voice. We've just been conditioned by our fears to believe we do not have one. Our parents didn't consciously condition that fear into us. They just didn't know better. They were conditioned that way as well. Society conditions us, generation after generation, and until we can be strong and break that pattern, we will remain voiceless! It's so simple to exercise my God-given right to speak up. And the most important thing is to always speak from LOVE. Set the example for everyone else that we must always speak from LOVE! In the current crisis, our world is in, we must step up and express our voice to support not only the highest, greatest good of ourselves, but also for EVERYONE!

LOVE IS THE ANSWER! It sounds so simple, yet truth is always simple.

Love is the Answer is a song by England Dan and John Ford Coley, and it was one of Gary's favorites. I loved being intuitively reminded through the writing exercise about this song! I decided to begin a daily game on my Facebook page called Love Is the Answer. It was for fifteen days, and each day I did a live video where I shared an intention from my spiritual teacher and how I interpreted that intention for me. I created an image for each day with the intention on it. It was a great way to keep up my energy, as I supported others in keeping up theirs during this challenging time. It was a beautiful time to go within, to dream big dreams, and practice extreme self-care. I was grateful to be alive and aware!

As the lockdown continued, we began to think of creative ways to spend the days. Mom had a box full of puzzles, and we did all of them. We bought word searches and crossword puzzle books to keep our minds stimulated. We read books. Then we took online piano lessons, as mom had two keyboards stored in the basement. We took daily walks to get fresh air and be nurtured by nature. Being in quarantine was showing us the simple, shared way of life! There is good in everything! I got a flashback to being at the Anne Frank Museum the previous September and was grateful that we were not confined indoors.

It's early April, and we have completed nine piano lessons. It's confusing, all the music theory stuff! Mom is doing way better than I, but she practices more. When things don't come easily for me, I lose interest quickly. I was challenged with getting and staying motivated. I had things I could do for my business, but with so many things up in the air, it was hard to stay focused.

I was creating more videos for my Facebook page. I began my Inner Garden series, based on my daily walks. I found interesting things during these walks that helped spur my creativity. Mom and I visited many local parks around the neighborhood. One day we walked around a lake that my mom used to visit as a child. Back then, it was a long drive from her home in Denver. Now it was in the suburb she lived in. I recorded my Groundhog Day video on this walk. I realized that waking up every day during a pandemic was very much like waking up every day after Gary died. Each new day was a repeat of the day before. I would wake up each morning and realize that the pandemic was still here.

Just like waking up and realizing that Gary was still dead. Ugh, what do I do now?

I was reminded of the movie "Groundhog Day" with Bill Murray and shared this on the video. He was stuck on the same day, every day, with no power to change it. Then he realized that he could do something different every day and that he did have power. At first, he did mean things. Then over time, he began to do nice things. The pandemic was causing grief for everyone. We'd lost our normal routines, many of us lost our jobs, and some lost family and friends to the virus. Grief is the same regardless of how it comes about. And just like Bill Murray in the movie, we can do something different every day to break the monotony, to remind us that we have a choice. And in that choice lies our power.

It's late April, and life in a pandemic is a weird combination of duality. Time drags, and time flies, all at the same time. I'm learning a lot about myself in the world. I began to think about writing a book about my year of travel and how it helped with my grieving. I would also weave in flashbacks from Gary's life and quotes from his journal. I was using some of the same tools now during the pandemic, and an idea percolated about tying them together in the book. I discussed it with my business coach, and she loved it. During a group coaching call, my coach called on me to share my progress. It was good to say it out loud again. After the call, I took a walk and recorded my book introduction! It came so easily! Over the next two days, I put the outline together. I loved how it was evolving.

In early May, with no money coming in, mom and I became InstaCart shoppers. It was good to get money flowing back in, and it was fun to get out of the house and shop. We enjoyed helping others: young mothers with babies, the elderly, people with immune challenges, and those who chose to stay home and be safe.

I committed to writing my book! I submitted my outline and introduction to my publisher. They eagerly accepted it and said it was so powerful. She even said, "I want this book in my life!" Such strong words of acceptance! I was determined to write this book for Gary and for me. My original completion dates were long past; however, I knew that things happen when they are meant to happen. There was obviously a bit more to include in the book than there was in my original timeline!

One of my events that went virtual was originally supposed to be in Seattle. As the host, my job was to secure the venue and be the onsite event manager. As this was now virtual, my duties were much fewer, and I was just required to kick-off the event each day and close it at the end. I recorded three videos, and I got to experience my first virtual hosting event. It was a great experience.

Mom and I began to put a plan into place. We decided to put her condo on the market, with the hopes of heading back to Washington by the end of May. Then we would head to Florida in July or August and sell my townhouse and buy a bigger house for my daughter and us. Then we planned to spend time between Washington, Colorado, and Florida. We were excited about new adventures.

Flashback: June 2018

On Friday morning, June 1, the hospice nurses arrived. They checked Gary's vitals and determined that it would not be long. The hospital bed and other supplies arrived at 3:15 p.m. We placed the bed upstairs next to his chair, and I prepared the bedding. The supplies included adult diapers, and I held one up and said to his brother: "This is exactly what he didn't want to have happen." As we lifted him up from his chair and carried him the short distance to the bed, his body released urine. I was rattled as I stepped in it in my socks. Once we laid him down, I quickly cleaned the carpet. His brother cleaned him up, and then we rolled him side to side as we removed the soiled sheets and replaced them with clean ones. As I was carrying the soiled sheets down the stairs, his brother said I should come back up. I dropped the sheets in the washer and quickly went back upstairs. Gary was gone. I had heard that people will wait until their loved ones leave before they die. I assumed that Gary wanted to let go and spare me the pain of witnessing it. And he shared that last moment with his little brother, who later told me that it was a gentle passing. That he just took in a final deep breath and left on the exhale.

As I sat with his body, I said my goodbyes and sent his Spirit off with all my love. His left eye was partly open. I attempted to close it, but it remained open. As I looked into his beautiful blue left eye, I saw a sparkle, and I knew he was still with me. That was his way of saying goodbye. A memory came to mind of an event in Cancun. We were cleaning up, and I was on stage with the microphone. I had our AV guy play the Carpenter's song, *Close To You*, and began singing it to Gary. He was so embarrassed! I thought of the lyrics that said: *On the day that you were born, the angels got together and decided to create a dream come true, So they sprinkled moon dust in your hair of gold and starlight in your eyes of blue.* I mentioned in a previous chapter about a psychic reading I had in January 2019. One of the things that Gary said to the psychic was to remind me about something I noticed about his eyes when he died!

Two days after he passed, I drove to a massage appointment. While driving, I got a message in my head saying, you need to connect with TG. TG is Gary's daughter, who he had sadly lost touch with years before. I decided to connect with her as soon as my massage was finished, and guess who messaged me during my massage? TG! Gary had reached out to her too. He couldn't voice his love here, and she couldn't hear him here, yet he was able to connect once he passed! And she was ready to listen.

The day she told me, "I think we can fix this now that he's on the other side," was so profound. For me, this answered the question of why Gary couldn't heal himself. The sacrifice that we had to make with his death was worth it for him and his daughter to be united again—and now I have another beautiful daughter in my life, my children have a wonderful older sister, and my mom has another granddaughter!

What Are The Gifts?

Life is filled with endless opportunities to learn and grow. Many of these opportunities come from the challenges, tragedies, and breakdowns that we experience throughout our lives. There are so many things to be grateful for, even in the face of devastating loss.

When we ask ourselves, "What is this loss teaching me?" we make a divine choice to see the bigger picture. We open our hearts to understanding and acceptance. By opening our hearts in this way, we affirm our self-love so we can light the way for others.

Every day now, I am aware of my connection to Spirit. Many times, whenever I think of Gary, a sign will appear or a knowing comes. I've learned that there is a gift in everything that happens to us, good or bad.

I've also realized that nothing is a lost cause. Relationships or experiences that don't meet our expectations are opportunities to question our expectations. Are they realistic? Do they serve us? Could there be other, higher reasons that they are not realized? Anytime I am confused or angry, I start asking myself the tough questions, the scary questions. I find the questions are what brings forth the insight. And that insight can then be examined from an objective place. Then I can take decisive action from my own place of power.

Activity: Different Dare

- What can you do to move forward? Don't get caught up in the Groundhog Day scenario. Remember how Bill Murray's character realized that he could change things by doing something different?
- Create a list of different things you can do every day, big or small. Doing a word search puzzle, driving a

new way to work, taking a walk, listening to music, journaling, singing, dancing, etc. Anything that raises your energy and makes you feel good!

- Each day choose one thing from the list and do it!

Gratitude, Laughter, Divine

Think about today, and answer these questions in your journal:

- What are you grateful for today?
- What made you laugh today?
- Did you feel the Divine today?

Epilogue: Through & Forward
June-December 2020

Gary Shares: "I am able to shine and contribute, and the joy that I feel resonates to all that I love and beyond."

Mom and I decided to head to downtown Denver to experience the peaceful protests that followed the not-so-peaceful protests. As we parked our car downtown, a yellow butterfly greeted us. As we walked around the capitol building, another yellow butterfly flew near us. It was sad to see the defacing of the capitol and other beautiful buildings and monuments. I know the buildings represent government, but they are also beautiful artistic examples of creativity and inspiration. They didn't deserve to be desecrated. It was eerie to walk around the 16th Street Mall, with few people around and many businesses boarded up. It reminded me of how we put up our own walls and hide from others in our grief. It stirred up my fears of being isolated and unseen, of mayhem and catastrophe around every corner. I allowed myself to feel these emotions bubbling up, and then I remembered the yellow butterfly that was awaiting us as we arrived. It was a reminder to remember the beauty in all things, even the desecration of buildings. We diminish our bodies in the same way when we don't practice compassion and care for ourselves. Being aware is the first step in allowing that negative energy to move out of our bodies. Remembering the Divine, a yellow butterfly, is allowing the good energy to lovingly fill that newly vacated space.

In mid-June, I flew back to Washington State on Alaska Airlines. I was confident in their safety precautions during the trip, and it was good to be home after being away for over three months due to the pandemic. It hit me again as we landed at SeaTac that Gary was gone. It was like so many other trips home, realizing he still would not be there to greet me and take care of me. All the pain, anger, and sadness surfaced again. The house was in the disarray that I left it in so many months ago, as I had not anticipated I would be gone so long. It was only supposed to be a couple of weeks. I was in the process of decluttering and re-organizing, so while sheltering in place in Denver, getting my mind clear and figuring out my business options, my house, my past, and Washington were left in limbo. I came back to stacks of papers that needed to be tended to. There were event supplies that were no longer needed due to the event ban. Do I store them for the future? Is there even a future for live events? Should I just let them go, for now, knowing that if it does come back, and I decide that's still my passion, I can get new supplies?

I also came back to take care of some financial stuff. And most importantly, to see my son, Hera, and Gizmo!

It's been raining here in Rainier the entire time I've been back. Like the universe is saying to me, don't save anything for a rainy day, because then every day might be raining! Take care of what needs to be done and cleared now, while being present. Clear it with love and grace and gratitude for all it brought me. Things and trinkets that no longer serve me, let them go in the same way. Don't be afraid that letting them go negates my life with Gary. I'll never have that back. He would want me to move forward unencumbered. It's time to get moving, to find my true purpose, and to find my passion and my joy.

I love that I speak to him every day as if he's here, and I do believe he is here in Spirit. I see it in the signs. I know he doesn't hold any resentment for what I could've done better. He would want me to take what I learned about my experience and create anew based on that.

After two weeks, I returned to Denver, just in time for the 4th of July holiday. As I watched the fireworks in our neighborhood, I felt such amazing energy for better days to come. There were people shooting off big and very loud fireworks all around us. My mom and I ventured outside, and we were instantly immersed in a 360-surround-sound of booms, crackles, and the oohs and aahs of everyone experiencing, for a few moments, the freedom we all deserve. I feel we are on the precipice of something BIG! The Universe has our backs, and God is watching over us and celebrating with us. Let's continue to be safe while expressing our true voices. Let Freedom Ring!

In mid-July, mom and I flew to Jacksonville with plans to sell my townhouse there. My daughter had been officially laid off from the Hyatt, so we changed our plans of buying a bigger home in Florida. Instead, we moved her to Denver. The townhouse went on the market on July 24th, and within a couple days, we got a full-price offer. We closed on August 24th and hit the road on August 29th. We spent a couple days in Tampa, visiting with family. On September 1st, we were

173

back on the road. We made a side trip to Selma, Alabama, to drive across the Edmund Pettus Bridge. On September 2nd, we drove through Louisiana and Texas. On September 3rd, we crossed into New Mexico, and the following day we arrived in Denver.

One of the homework tasks in a spiritual group I belong to was to focus on a loved one and ask for signs. The day happened to be August 19th, which would have been Gary's 65th birthday. It was extra special, and I got four signs! The best one was my new niece being born. We spent the day in the pool, and there was a dragonfly that spent several minutes with us, divebombing the water near us and flying over our heads like a fighter jet. I had ordered a feather hand-painted with a hummingbird several weeks ago, and it arrived on this day. Later as we all took a walk, I found two pennies. One was dated 1990, the year my daughter was born, and she just turned 30 on the 13th. The other was dated 1973, the year Gary graduated high school. So many wonderful synchronicities celebrating Gary's birthday!

With everything that was going on in the political arena, I decided to launch a video campaign on September 1st called the Elevated States of America. As I watched the online Democratic and Republican National Conventions, I LOVED the roll call with all 50 states, the District of Columbia, and the US territories: a total of 56 places. It was so refreshing to see people just like me, in an elevated state of pride and joy, answering the call! I had an inspiring idea: for the next 56 days, we would learn about each of these places. Simple and fun facts put together in a short video about each state/territory. The campaign ran through November 1st. My goal was celebrating 'US the people' in the USA, not the politics! Regardless of party preferences or presidential choice, we are all still citizens of an amazing country with incredible diversity and beauty!

After two failed contracts on my mom's condo in Colorado, we took it off the market and decided to drive to Washington. On October 24th, we packed up the truck and took I-25 north through Wyoming. We veered east a bit into South Dakota, as we wanted to see Mount Rushmore and the Crazy Horse Memorial. A winter storm rolled in as we arrived at Crazy Horse, and we could barely see it. They extended our pass for the next day, and we headed into Keystone, just past Mount Rushmore. Most everything was closed for the season, but we did find a room at the Roosevelt Hotel. There were many quotes from President Theodore Roosevelt on the walls, and this one resonated with me: *People don't care how much you know, until they know how much you care.*

The next morning, the snow had stopped, but it was a winter wonderland! We slowly made our way to Mount Rushmore, and just past the sign, the monument was nearly right in front of us! We pulled over to take pictures. We then made our way to the memorial, paid our fee, and walked down the long flag-lined pathway that led to the monument. It was spectacular! We then went back to Crazy Horse and witnessed this amazing creation. It was so worth traveling through the inclement weather to stand before such awe-inspiring artistry.

We took a little side road when we saw the sign for Devil's Tower. Anyone who grew up in the '70s should remember the movie, *Close Encounters of the Third Kind.*

There's a scene where Richard Dreyfuss is eating dinner with his family, and he uses all the mashed potatoes to make a replica of Devil's Tower. I just had to see it for myself! We learned at the Crazy Horse museum that the Native American Crow legend about the tower was that a giant bear was chasing two sisters. As they escaped onto a rock, it grew out of the ground remarkably high. The bear attempted to reach them, and the vertical lines all around the tower were carved by the bear's claws.

As we drove into Montana, we stopped at the site in Darby where they film the show "Yellowstone." Mom is a huge fan of Kevin Costner. We tried to get a picture, but the guard would not allow us near it. Dejected, we made our way to Lake Como in the Bitterroot National Forest, which was truly breathtaking. It took away the bitter sting of being snubbed by the Yellowstone crew! We crossed the state line into Idaho and stopped to see another beautiful setting, Lake Coeur d'Alene. Much later that evening, we were grateful to be home! We were stressed by the winter weather, especially the icy conditions and having to stop every so often and chip away the thick ice that built up so fast in the wheel wells.

I decided to sell the house that Gary and I shared for 21 years. The house where he created amazing rock beds and gardens within the five acres. Where he did beautiful tile work and painting techniques on the inside. The front two-thirds was where the house sat. The back third was a wild forest, where occasional trillium flowers bloomed. Deer roamed through the property, eating up our many plants until we learned which ones were deer-proof. We routinely saw raccoons and possums and occasionally heard coyote packs. The spring rains brought the deafening frog chorus that played at dusk in the seasonal pond. It was a beautiful piece of heaven. And for this suburban girl, it was a lot to maintain without Gary. We bought this place because Gary wanted to be in the country with land around him. I had agreed because I just wanted to be wherever he was.

My mom and I had broached the subject of moving to Colorado with my son a few times. He always said no. On November 8th, my mom asked him again. This time he agreed! He was ready for a new adventure! Within one hour of his decision, I contacted a local realtor. I had already considered selling it soon after Gary died. I had even discussed it with Gary. He told me he was fine with whatever I decided to do. The only misgiving I had was that no one would appreciate Gary's work. I feared the beautiful rock gardens would fall into disrepair without someone who knew and loved him and knew how much love and energy he had put into them. As soon as my son made his decision, I tuned into Gary, and a feeling of peace came over me. I knew that he was giving me his blessing to move on.

November 12th marked my 57th birthday. It was hard to believe I was celebrating my third birthday without Gary. As a complement to this book, I wrote a meditation for death and loss. I had attempted many times to record it myself in a closet and then a bathroom. The sound quality just wasn't right. I celebrated my birthday by driving to Seattle and recording the meditation in a real live recording studio! My mom came with me, but I asked her to stay outside. I was too nervous about having anyone with me. The recording engineer really loved the meditations! Afterward, we made our way to Pike Place Market for a celebration salmon lunch!

We quickly got the house ready, and it went on the market the Friday after Thanksgiving. We had three showings on Saturday and one on Sunday. We received an offer a few days later from the Sunday showing, for several thousand dollars over the asking price! Our house was officially under contract. We had a lot of work to prepare for the move, as we had over 23 years of accumulation to deal with. We had two old Volvos on the property that hadn't run in years. The red sedan was the car Gary drove when I met him, and I can still remember him driving this car. He had refurbished it himself. There was also a green wagon that he had given up refurbishing years ago. I called the local wrecking yard, and they came within the hour and took both cars. It was sad to see them leaving the property. My mom and I both watched with teary eyes. I took pictures of each one as they rolled down the driveway.

I started selling lots of things online, as we didn't plan to take everything with us. One of the biggest things to sell was Gary's woodworking tools. There were four big pieces of equipment. I posted them all on Offer Up and had only sold one. I then posted them on Craigslist. The retired contractor whom Gary bought the tools from years ago emailed me after seeing the tools on Craigslist! After RVing for a few years, he and his wife had bought a house in Oregon. He was looking for tools, and he bought back the three that were left! They were so sweet and incredibly sad that Gary died. He was extremely happy to get his tools back, as he built their last house with them. He said, "I may never get them set up, but it's just nostalgic to have them back." It was so comforting for me. I'm sure Gary made it happen!

Due Diligence AND Do Difference

According to Wikipedia, the term "due diligence" means "required carefulness" or "reasonable care" in general usage. As a common business term, due diligence is the process of "reasonable investigation." There's also the action part, which is taking the steps required to move forward. I believe it's important to practice due diligence every day. What this means in the grief arena is the required carefulness of our heart and mind, the reasonable care of our body, and a daily game plan of the steps we need to take to move forward into joy.

Part of that daily game plan should be "do difference," a "required novelness" that we enact daily. It means doing something different every day. It could be as simple as driving to the store on a different route, choosing a new affirmation from a card deck, or watching a TV show you've never watched. It could be more challenging, like trying a new recipe, doing a juice cleanse, playing a game, or researching a subject that inspires you. Doing something different every day is called a pattern interrupt. It trips the mind from its current path onto another path that will open doorways to other experiences that are not part of the usual pattern. That spark of inspiration reveals new possibilities. It puts us in a state of expansion, where we can learn new skills to move through our grief. Eventually, with consistent practice, we can move beyond our grief. This doesn't mean that the grief goes away; it just entrains us to navigate more gracefully through it when it arises.

While I was on my year of travel after Gary died, I had trouble letting go and enjoying each day. I spent a lot of time analyzing my schedule, planning future trips, and taking care of those around me. Anything to keep my mind busy to push down my grief and sadness, which took me out of being present and enjoying the moment.

The present moment is where we can heal our emotional traumas by allowing a feeling to be felt with the sole intention of moving through it. This is different than sulking and feeling sorry for ourselves in the present moment, which only serves to maintain that state of loss. The present moment is also where we find happiness and joy. It sounds like a contradiction, but when we are aware of our emotional status in the present moment, and we don't stuff it down, we can then move through it into happiness and joy. It takes a lot of work, but it's well worth the effort. Over time, it becomes easier to stay in the present moment for longer periods of time.

A few months into my journey, I came up with a daily practice, which I dubbed the Day Tripper Challenge. I mentioned this in a previous chapter, but here's a little more detail. Day Tripper refers to a song by my favorite band, The Beatles, and it was appropriate because I liked the idea that each day, I could trip my mind into being present by looking for three things that were most important to my well-being. I posted them daily to my Facebook page. Journaling is also a great way to practice this technique.

The three things I look for: *Gratitude, Laughter, Divine*

This activity is about everyday reverence and having a *GLaD* day! You've been practicing this at the end of every chapter. Now it's time to make it part of your daily routine.

Here is a link for the journal I created for this practice: www.gpeventworx.com/journal

Our bodies, just like science, are self-correcting. In each moment, we don't know what we don't know. We make decisions based on what we do know. We base our actions on the data we have at the time. As we grow and evolve, we learn more, and that new learning helps us course correct. As Maya Angelou said, *"When we know better, we do better."*

I believe that the death of a loved one can cause PTSD. Whether we watch our loved one die due to an illness or an unexpected death, we relive those moments over and over. For me, I had a hard time getting the images of my severely diminished husband out of my head. All I wanted was to remember him at his most vibrant, but I could not get past those horrific images. To make things worse, I had taken photos of him after he died. I don't know why. I just felt compelled to. For many months, I left those images in my camera roll. When I would scroll through to find a picture, I would inadvertently see those images of my dead husband, and it would trigger the pain just as intensely as if it just happened. The emotions were crushing. I kept telling myself that I needed to move those photos to another folder to avoid the trigger. Yet, I couldn't get myself to do it. It felt like that would be erasing Gary's existence.

While visiting a friend whose son had just passed away, I shared with her about the photos. She didn't think it was odd at all, but her first suggestion was to file them somewhere else! Once somebody else voiced that option, I could take it seriously. It's funny how we don't listen to our own knowingness. That's why it's essential to surround ourselves with people who empathize and understand our experience. People who can support us in loving ways to ease us through the grieving process.

Grief affects everyone. I am an expert on grief. You are an expert on grief. We all have experienced loss; therefore, we've all been touched by grief. Some have been very tragic, others might be middle of the road, and others are short-lived and easily manageable. When I say we're all experts, let me clarify that you can be an expert in grief in four phases.

One phase overwhelms you and makes life difficult. You find yourself wallowing in the pain. I was an expert at this level at one point.

A similar phase is just as overwhelming, except that you stuff the grief down and pretend you're okay. This can be very damaging to your body. I was a super expert at this one.

Another phase doesn't drown you, but it keeps you barely afloat. You just keep treading water but get nowhere. I'm also an expert at that.

Still, another phase is managing it, moving through it, and ultimately moving beyond it. That is the harder phase of grief to become an expert at, but it definitely is achievable. I'm an expert at that as well.

We can be experts in all four phases. When the big tides of grief wash over us, we can pull from each area of expertise to help us get through it.

As many of you are aware and have experienced, you can feel like you're doing great, and then something triggers you. You go from feeling at the top of your game then quickly find yourself at the bottom of the well. It happens, and it's okay, but that doesn't mean you have to stay there. You can draw on your reserves from these four phases and remember what it took to move through them.

I hold the power. I created me. Not the people or experiences in my life. I have the power to say yes or no when an experience or person presents itself. If I say yes, I get one version of that experience. If I say no, I get another version of that experience. Ultimately the power holder is not the person or experience. It's ME!

Rather than let grief drown me, I'm choosing to let grief save me. I'm choosing to see and understand that there's a gift in it. That I created this reality to further my growth. I choose the people and experiences in my life to further my growth. I take responsibility for everything that happens. I choose to see the bigger picture, that everything happens for a reason. We are not accidents of our environment.

By taking my power back, I can create even better experiences and attract quality people into my life. When I get depressed about people, places, and things that are no longer part of my life, I remember my power. I acknowledge them for shaping me to become who I am. I have mercy on them for their part in my experience. I'm grateful for them because the experience has helped me learn about extending mercy to others.

I trust God. I trust my Spirit family. Most importantly, I trust myself. Sometimes that trust in myself wavers because that's what we do as humans. Ultimately, to live the best version of my life, I must trust in myself. I must trust in my Spirit team and know that there's a bigger plan. Everything that's happened to me is part of the path to that bigger plan, and it couldn't happen without those things. The lesson for me is to allow myself to feel the feelings when they come up, but don't stay there. Allow them, acknowledge them, think about them, ask them what they're here to teach me, and then thank them for their participation. Thank them for their energy. Thank them for a wonderful enactment of the experience. Then I gain wisdom when I see the gifts. I move through and forward into a better version of me.

I love traveling, and being unable to travel due to Covid-19 has been hard for me! I found travel to be the best way to open my heart and mind to the possibility that I could be happy again. We only need to be present and conscious and allow joy in! It's always there. I'm confident that there are more travels to come. It's interesting how I completed my year of travel that started nine months after my husband's death and ended with a global pandemic! In that time of glorious freedom followed by challenging confinement, I learned so much about life, about death, and that happiness and joy are always possible.

The key to moving forward after a devastating loss is to create a new future. To create experiences NOW that will be beautiful memories in the future! By consciously creating our future memories NOW that are joyful and filled with potential, we can gently place them alongside the beautiful memories of our loved ones and step into a renewed excitement for life and all its beautiful, unlimited poss-ibilities!

Becoming a widow at 54 was a huge shock to my system. Yet from the chaos, a new life presented itself, like a phoenix rising from the ashes. I'm being presented with new ideas in life, things that I would have never considered before widowhood arrived. Out of the shards of my former existence emerges a new way of being, a new existence filled with pain and pleasure at the same time. I am learning to convert the energy of pain and loss into the energy of love and joy. Understanding why some people fall away and are even cruel is a lesson in the art and beauty of humanity. It is possible to be happy again!

Living in this world is about the balance between life and death, sorrow and joy, pain and healing, loss and discovery, give and take, love and hate, illness and wellness, dark and light. These lessons are a continual way to hone your soul, to emerge the hero, to rise above, and ultimately, to gain the ability to transform the energy of loss into the energy of wisdom with ease and grace. Every setback is an opportunity gifted to us by Spirit to learn the art of conscious unraveling and stepping into conscious creation. Being conscious through the process allows us to see the gift in the chaos. There is always a gift! We should always be asking the bigger questions: What is the lesson in this situation? What is being presented? What does the universe want me to know?

Grief is a crazy thing. Sometimes all is well, and sometimes all is not well. It never goes away, but like anything, it can be transformed. I've chosen to see the good things about my experience with Gary. I still have emotional moments, but I don't let them last as long. I choose to move beyond the tragedy and become powerful because of it.

It is also immensely helpful to be around people who are experiencing the same thing. The key is choosing wisely. I don't want to be around people who lament and are angry and can't see their part in the life they chose.

I remember Gary's gift: his essence. He's not a body, but a loving being, a powerful force for good. He's always with me. His illness was a great lesson for his progress. I see him radiantly healthy. His illness was not who he was. Although it emaciated his body, it could never diminish or compromise his true essence. I remember his love. He's more alive now than he ever was here.

My spiritual teacher presented me with my angel and word for 2021. How appropriate that it's Archangel Gabriel, the angel of communication! I've asked him for guidance a lot while writing this book. And my word is alignment, perfect as I continue my journey to align body, mind, and spirit.

This is my next and greatest adventure in the evolution of my soul. Death is a great teacher, and it can pull you under. Yet, it can show you the cosmos if you allow it to unfold. Death is a door into another world, one that allows your loved one to keep moving forward into their next great adventure while at the same time providing you with a new way of navigating in this world. It's up to you how everything unfolds, will it unfold in happiness or will it unfold in despair? Only you can make that choice. Yes, YOU! You are that powerful!

Join me, and let's create magic together!

Made in United States
Orlando, FL
14 July 2022

19773940R00114